How to get the best graduate job

PEARSON
Prentice Hall
BUSINESS

Books that make you better

Books that make you better. That make you *be* better, *do* better, *feel* better. Whether you want to upgrade your personal skills or change your job, whether you want to improve your managerial style, become a more powerful communicator, or be stimulated and inspired as you work.

Prentice Hall Business is leading the field with a new breed of skills, careers and development books. Books that are a cut above the mainstream – in topic, content and delivery – with an edge and verve that will make you better, with less effort.

Books that are as sharp and smart as you are.

Prentice Hall Business.
We work harder – so you don't have to.

For more details on products, and to contact us, visit
www.pearsoned.co.uk

How to get the best graduate job

Insider strategies for success in the graduate job market

David Williams, Phil Brown and Anthony Hesketh

PEARSON

Prentice Hall

BUSINESS

Harlow, England • London • New York • Boston • San Francisco • Toronto • Sydney • Tokyo • Singapore • Hong Kong
Seoul • Taipei • New Delhi • Cape Town • Madrid • Mexico City • Amsterdam • Munich • Paris • Milan

PEARSON EDUCATION LIMITED

Edinburgh Gate
Harlow CM20 2JE
Tel: +44 (0)1279 623623
Fax: +44 (0)1279 431059
Website: www.pearsoned.co.uk

First published in Great Britain in 2006

© David Williams, Phil Brown and Anthony Hesketh 2006

The rights of David Williams, Phil Brown and Anthony Hesketh to be identified as authors of this work have been asserted by them in accordance with the copyright, Designs and Patents Act 1988.

ISBN 13: 978-0-273-70355-6
ISBN-10: 0-273-70355-2

British Library Cataloguing-in-Publication Data
A catalogue record for this book is available from the British Library

Library of Congress Cataloging-in-Publication Data
Williams, David, 1966–
    How to get the best graduate job : insider strategies for success in the graduate job market / David Williams, Phil Brown and Anthony Hesketh.
        p. cm.
    ISBN-13: 978-0-273-70355-6 (alk. paper)
    ISBN-10: 0-273-70355-2 (alk. paper)
        1. Job hunting. 2. College graduates—Employment. 3. School-to-work transition.
    I. Hesketh, Anthony. II. Brown, Phillip, 1957– III. Title.

    HF5382.7.W49 2006
    650.14—dc22

                                                                            2005053517

10 9 8 7 6 5 4 3 2 1
09 08 07 06 05

Typeset in 10pt Iowan by 70
Printed and bound in Great Britain by Henry Ling Ltd, at the Dorset Press, Dorchester, Dorset

The Publisher's policy is to use paper manufactured from sustainable forests.

Contents

About the authors

Phillip Brown and Anthony Hesketh are political economists. Their original research into the graduate market has been featured in *The Times, Daily Mail, Times Higher Education Supplement* and *Western Mail*.

David Williams is a writer who has been reporting on graduate recruitment and the marketing of graduate vacancies for over a decade.

Introduction

Have you heard this one?

> A certain company is used to getting so many applications that it throws half of them unexamined into the bin, on the rationale that 'we don't employ unlucky people'.

Or this one?

> There's a story about a company that when you walk into an interview room there isn't a chair for you to sit on – it's sort of an intelligence test, who asks for a chair and who does the interview while standing up?

Or this?

> Someone told me the other day – it's probably an urban myth – but this big organization, when they had assessment centres, years ago the candidates would walk into dinner and whoever put salt on their food they'd send them straight home.

You have probably heard these stories or variations on them lots of times. They make up the underground view of graduate recruitment. According to these myths – and we are pretty sure they are myths (pretty sure) – the whole thing is about employers making arbitrary decisions based on inconsequential differences, or it's all just about luck, or it comes down to your response to an unreal situation in which both courses of action seem entirely reasonable. Do they want me to be assertive and ask for a chair? Or do they want me to be a team player and cooperate with their creative approach to the process – 'why yes, that's different, let's do the interview standing up!'

Despite their obviously not being true, the problem is that the myths are the first of only four sources of information that you have about graduate recruitment, and all of them are partial.

The four sources of information you have on graduate recruitment:

- myths
- candidate stories
- parental wisdom
- industry advice.

Candidate stories

The second source is what you hear from friends and friends of friends about how they have approached the whole thing. This anecdotal information will usually take one of two forms. It will either go something like this:

You know you have to just be who you are really. And if they are not looking for someone like you then well that is the best way to go into it I think. Just be yourself. There is no point in trying to model yourself on someone else you have met or whatever.

Or it might sound something like this:

All my really good friends have been telling me for ages that I've got to go along to interviews and basically *not* be myself. They are all more successful in interviews and things than I am and they all say you've got to go along and tell them what they want to hear.

This anecdotal source usually comes down to a simple question – how much should you be yourself?

Parental wisdom

If your parents went to university, they might provide the third source of information. However, as valuable as their insights might be, we will see at the beginning of Part 1 how a lot has changed since your parents' day. So, without suggesting that their advice might be limited to other areas of your life, it might be a good idea to ask them to read this book before they contribute further.

Industry advice

The final source of information comes from the recruitment industry itself. This is the official version, and it is promoted by the employers, by the consultants who design the application forms and assessment centres, by the university careers services, and by the graduate recruitment magazines and websites. Together, all of these make up what is known as the graduate recruitment industry. The following is an amalgam of the sort of advice you will have heard many times before.

When it comes to the assessment centre, try to relax and be yourself. It's difficult of course, but the various tests and interviews have been designed to match the best candidate to the job. If you try to pretend to be someone else, or if you try to present yourself as the ideal candidate you think they are looking for, you are likely to do very badly. The assessors are wise to these sorts of tricks and will almost certainly see through any sort of performance.

The first problem with these four sources is the way that they contradict each other. The myths say it's all arbitrary while the industry claims the results are objective. The official advice sources (probably along with your parents) tell you to be yourself, while some of your peers are telling you to act up to what the assessors want to see. Trying to find a path through all this contradictory advice is not easy.

The second problem is that all this information is partial. The myths are not true of course. Your friends might have been to assessment centres, but their recollections of what happened there and how they managed to cope during some of the most pressured hours of their lives are not necessarily the most objective basis on which to build a strategy. Your parents will not understand how much has changed, and while there is a lot of very valuable advice which is made freely available by the recruitment industry, you should never forget that there is a reason this information is free. All the websites and careers magazines you use are paid for by employers through vacancy advertising and so they can never say anything that is too critical of the methods employers use.

What this book provides – the fifth dimension: a new source of information

We *can* be critical however. What this book offers is a completely new source of information about graduate recruitment. We can make this claim because two of the authors are the only independent observers ever to have gone into assessment centres and to have analyzed what actually happens during the selection process.* As part of a four-year academic study, we talked at length to employers and candidates, sat in on final interviews, watched the tests and group activities being conducted, and were even present during the private, post-assessment 'washing-up' sessions when the employers made the final decision about which candidates would get a job offer. For the first time, this enables us to give a completely independent view of how graduate recruitment really works. Instead of having to rely on partial information from the recruitment industry and from other graduates, this book provides the first truly independent, authoritative guide to getting a good graduate job.

The fact that we are independent observers enables us to tell you things that the graduate recruitment industry cannot. For example, if you are applying, not getting interviews, and

* This book draws on the results of an Economic and Social Research Council funded project (Ref: 00239101), some of which were published in *The Mismanagement of Talent* (Philip Brown and Anthony Hesketh with Sara Williams, Oxford University Press, 2004).

suspect that there is a magic formula to writing application forms that no one is telling you, this book can help (there *is* a magic formula and we will show you what it is). We can also show you why all the other sources of information are so contradictory. For example, in some ways the myths are right. There are undoubtedly points in the graduate recruitment process when tiny, apparently inconsequential differences between candidates are used to separate the winners from the losers. We will show you when this happens, how it happens, and what significance it has for your chances of being picked. On the other hand, we also know that there are times when you should place your trust in what the employers are claiming. Parts of this process *are* objective. There are points when your capabilities are being rationally assessed, the results then being used to properly distinguish people who can do the job from those who cannot. We will tell you when this happens and how you can alter your chances of success.

Perhaps most controversially, we can also help you answer the vital question of whether it pays to be yourself. All the official advice you have ever read will tell you that the best strategy to adopt on the day is to try to be as true to yourself as you can (within the constraints of normal formality). The recruitment industry will tell you that the assessors can see through you if you try to fake it, that only being yourself will allow the objective assessment techniques to match your abilities to those required on the job, that, if you were to slip through, you wouldn't enjoy the work because you wouldn't be suited to it. However, having interviewed dozens of assessment centre candidates, it is obvious that, despite all the official exhortations not to do so, large numbers of graduates are playing a presentational game and some are getting away with it. Although being your best-behaved self is still a good strategy, all graduates should know that, as long as you can do it well, there appear to be no detrimental effects to your success, at least in the short term, in pretending to be someone you are not.

Throughout this book you are going to find lots of quotes from employers and candidates. Although we are not able to identify these sources directly (due to the contractual assurances that allowed us to engage in frank discussion with graduates and employers and to get inside the assessment centres in the first place), these are genuine quotes from real graduate recruitment managers and actual candidates. They are not the official words of the recruitment brochures nor the partial recollections of candidates trying to remember what happened to them in the pressure-cooker atmosphere of the assessment centre. The quotes come from lengthy, structured interviews that were conducted either at the assessment centres or within a short period of them taking place. The quotes will show you what employers are really thinking and what strategies and tactics other candidates are using to increase their chances of success.

How to use this book

Parts 2, 3 and 4 are the key sections in this book. They deal with the decision about where to apply, the application form and the assessment centre. These key chapters are the longest and each is divided into three subsections: 'Facts', 'Strategies' and 'Tactics'.

Facts, strategies . . .

The first subsection, 'The Facts', will give you the essential information you must take into account at that stage of the recruitment process, while 'The Strategies' will give you various approaches. We have done it this way because there are strategies that we know are being used successfully by graduates but which we cannot personally endorse.

Strategies are, of course, as much to do with the resources at your disposal as they are to do with the lie of the land. For example, some people will be comfortable with the idea of enhancing or concealing some aspects of themselves in order to impress employers, while other candidates would rather try to present a polished version of their real selves. The strategy subsection allows for these differences and shows you the advantages and disadvantages of each approach. Essentially, what this book does is give you the facts and then offer you the choices about how to deal with them. Ultimately, you must decide.

. . . and tactics

After this comes 'The Tactics'. This is much more like the sort of thing you will find in other careers books. Until we examined the process no one really knew how graduates were selected for the best jobs. All that graduate careers information could do was repeat the same basic tactics, most of which you probably already know: turn up with time to spare; dress appropriately; smile. The tactics section covers some of this, but what this book won't do is re-hash old information you can find very easily elsewhere. If you need to know how to write a curriculum vitae (CV) or how to answer a tricky interview question, you can get advice for free from careers services or on the web, or, of course, there are many useful books already available that cover this sort of information. What this book does is complement all the instructional guides by giving, for the first time, insights into what is really going on behind the scenes, both in terms of what employers want to see but cannot tell you and in terms of what strategies other graduates are successfully using.

Before and after

The first and last parts are a little different. Chapter 1 is simply called 'The facts you need to know' and takes you through the five factors that have combined to create the contemporary graduate jobs market. Although it might be tempting to skip this section and move to the heart of the book, you shouldn't; Chapter 1 provides the information that explains everything that follows. And it's short.

Finally there is Part 5. This looks at what happens afterwards. Those who have been offered graduate-to-management training contracts will obviously have their paths mapped out for them, at least for the next two to three years. But those who have not yet had an offer can find themselves in a limbo that can be very difficult to escape. Part 5, therefore, suggests some strategies for those who have not yet achieved their employment goal.

Perhaps more than anything, what this book can do is help you decide how you will approach the world of graduate recruitment. In some ways the decision to enter the market for these aspirational graduate jobs is one of the most important you can ever make, as is the choice of strategies and tactics you use. Success will take you into a different world from your peers and it will change almost everything about the life you will lead. It will affect your income and the things that derive from your income, such as the type of house and car you can afford. But it will also affect those subtler makers of your identity: how fulfilling you find work, your status in your family and among your friends, and even the sort of partner you might attract. Ultimately, however, success (or failure) in the graduate market also exacts a price. It can affect your sense of your own integrity, and even your sense of who you are. It is not just about strategies, tactics and winning or losing. The decision to enter the graduate market will bring you face to face with some deep questions concerning fairness, meritocracy and the nature of the self and of society. Graduate recruitment is a much stranger world than you might imagine. What follows will show you how it really works.

Part 1

CHAPTER 1

The facts you need to know

This is how it's supposed to work

Graduates from every university and from every ethnic and class background think seriously about who they are, their skills, the type of work they would enjoy, and the type of life they want. They look at the marketing done by employers, find those opportunities they think would suit them, and then they send off a few carefully targeted applications. Employers look through the applications, matching the qualifications and experiences the graduates possess against the knowledge and skills they know are required for the job. The best applicants are invited for an initial interview and then on to an assessment centre where, while giving the best impression that they can, they submit themselves to a range of objective methods of assessment that measure their potential to do well in that role and in that organization. The candidate who is most suitable for the needs of the organization is then offered the job.

This is the way most people still think that graduate recruitment works. The only thing that appears to have changed since your parents' day is the general adoption of the assessment centre as a final selection event. Having said that, if you were to read the previous paragraph out to someone who had been through a civil service or military recruitment process 25 or even 50 years ago they would think that nothing has changed. Most people think that graduate recruitment still works like this. Unfortunately they are mistaken. Almost everything about this characterization is wrong.

This is how it really works

Employers are so convinced they are in a war with each other for a limited supply of talented graduates that, despite lots of talk about attracting a diverse range of candidates, they concentrate their marketing on a relatively small number of universities in which they believe that talent is to be found. Students and graduates of those universities are able to use the insights provided by the marketing to gain an advantage over their peers at less prestigious universities, particularly in terms of understanding how to present themselves. Employers select those candidates who most convincingly present themselves in the right way for further examination at an initial interview and later at an assessment centre. Here employers and their recruitment consultants use a range of assessment tools that they believe accurately measure the hard and soft skills they know are required for the job. Despite this, they continue to make subjective judgements based on how well the candidates perform on the hard-to-measure soft skills. Some candidates have understood that some of the apparently objective measurements of their soft skills are really masking subjective assessments, and are prepared to manipulate as many aspects of themselves as they can in order to get the jobs. Other candidates either cannot do this or prefer not to and so concentrate on presenting their real selves. The candidates who offer the most convincing performance of what the employers want to see are the ones who get the job offers. There are likely to be many more suitable candidates than there are jobs. Employers, however, tend to maintain the fiction that they always recruit the best people and that the rejected candidates are in some way deficient.

The five key factors

To understand what has changed you need to know five key factors. Superficially, the old system and the new system are sufficiently similar for people to believe that nothing has really happened. However, beneath the surface, the underlying system has been warped and bent out of all recognition. The changes have been driven by five key factors. They are the graduate glut, the notion of a war for talent, the diversity agenda, the emergence of the knowledge brand, and the idea of self-actualization through work.

Factor one – the graduate glut

The graduate glut is the biggest factor that has changed graduate recruitment and it explains much of what follows. The glut is a simple phenomenon. Essentially it comes down to this: for every aspirational graduate job, UK universities produce about 20 graduates.

According to the Higher Education Statistics Agency (HESA), during the academic year 2003–4 the number of people who obtained higher education qualifications in the UK was 425,260. During the same year, the number of vacancies on offer by the blue chip members of the Association of Graduate Recruiters (AGR – the best guide available to the demand for top graduates) was 14,480. This is a ratio of graduates to aspirational jobs of over 29-to-1. Even when you exclude PhDs, holders of PGCEs and other vocational postgraduate qualifications, those with foundation degrees, higher national diplomas (HNDs) and other similar non-first-degree under-graduate qualifications, as well as all European Union (EU) and overseas graduates, from the total (although obviously some of these people will be competing for the same jobs) you still end up with 253,995 people gaining higher education qualifications in 2003–4. This lower figure still represents a ratio of over 17-to-1. None of this includes any of the university graduates who are already in the job market.

How the graduate glut has affected graduates

The graduate glut has created a situation in which 19 out of 20 (95 percent) of you are not going to get these aspirational graduate jobs. This has created a frenzy of competition in which some deeply held values concerning fair play and the nature of the self are being laid aside.

This is not just because aspirational jobs pay well (the average starting salary in an AGR job was £21,000 in 2004). Nor is it because they have good training programmes and are intellectually fulfilling (when you're in one, university doesn't feel like the end of your intellectual development; it should feel like the beginning). It isn't even because they make parents proud. The main reason graduate jobs are so valuable is because they have prospects.

It is obvious, but the reason employers spend so much time and money on campus-based marketing and assessment centres is because they want to find people who can handle being fast-tracked to positions of responsibility. Today's organizations are flatter than they once were; fat-cat-ism has concentrated more of the rewards towards the top: the higher up you go, the larger and more disproportionate a share of the organization's wealth becomes yours. The reason graduate training programmes are so prized is because they may be the best opportunity you ever have to fast-track yourself to real responsibility and the money that goes with it. Of course, talented people will get other breaks over time. Nevertheless, the biggest break you can ever have is to get yourself onto a graduate-to-management training scheme in your early twenties. What is more, getting one of these jobs will continue to pay off even if you hate it and leave after a year. Once one employer has shown a serious level of faith in your potential, another employer is more likely to do the same. The first job you get out of university is so important because it dictates what kind of job you can go on to next.

Given all this, it may be asking too much to expect your generation to play by the rules you inherited from previous generations of graduates. Today's graduate market is different. A very limited and valuable resource is being fought over by a far larger number of people, all of whom want and need it more or less as much. These jobs are just too valuable for all candidates to treat the application process as an exercise in personal development and so to focus their applications on a few carefully chosen organizations, although some continue to act as if this was the case. Despite both internal and external pressures, many candidates are not completely truthful about their suitability for a job, either on the application forms or in person at the assessment centres. The temptation to enhance aspects of your work experience, your personality, and even in some cases the qualifications you hold, is great and terrible. The biggest problem for today's graduates is that there is no agreed level as to how far this enhancement of the self can acceptably go. It is down to every individual to make a decision about how far along the path towards outright lying he or she is prepared to move.

The reason that you have to make this decision alone is not because you are part of a mendacious generation. It is simply because there is no guidance available to what is really happening (until this book of course). The graduate recruitment industry still presents itself as if nothing has changed. All you could do previously was listen to the myths, talk to your friends and try to figure out what it was about the official advice that sounded so wrong.

How the graduate glut has affected employers

The 20-to-1 ratio has not been that good for employers either. It has swamped them with applications, all of which, from their point of view, look more or less the same. If you look around at your peers, you will see that in employment terms most graduates are pretty equal. Mature students aside, you all have a degree, A-levels and GCSEs, and will almost certainly have some sort of part-time and/or temporary work experience. Possibly you will have been involved in some sort of voluntary activity and you may well have travelled abroad. This isn't much for employers to go on. They can look at the quality of your degree (subject, class and institution) and count your UCAS points. But with no past performance in a responsible job, no record at all to examine, all the employers can really do to tell you apart is look at the skills you have developed through your hobbies, your interests, and in the part-time and temporary jobs you have done. Beyond this, graduates are a blank slate. As we shall see, with nothing else to go on employers are forced into choosing between you on the basis of soft skills that have been picked up on your summer holidays, in your extra curricula and during your leisure activities. Picking future leaders on the basis of what they did in their summer holidays is not going to be easy.

This, then, is the graduate glut. It explains why some graduates behave as they do and why employers are so desperate to hear of situations in which your leadership skills made a difference.

Factor two – the war for talent

So if it is so difficult to choose between graduates, why do graduate recruiters bother? The answer is that they believe they are involved in a war for talent.

The whole of modern graduate recruitment is based on this concept. The war for talent is the belief that there are only a very few people who have the abilities to run complex modern organizations and make them excel. The only way these organizations can survive is to find these people before their rivals do. They have to be identified early and promoted rapidly if the organization is to capture them, keep them, and then benefit from their rare abilities.

Needless to say, top management loves the idea of the war for talent. Not only is the concept inherently flattering, it also provides an excellent justification for the enormous sums of money they are paid. Since everybody in these positions agrees they are all very special people who deserve special rewards, it is not difficult to convince them that they need a graduate programme which identifies people like them and singles them out for preferential training and promotion, and, of course, lots of money. In fact, in most cases, the more elitist the graduate programme the better, because the idea that an organization is hard to get into only increases the reputation of the people already in it.

Factor three – the diversity agenda

The war for talent is based on the idea of an elite. In order to get around the problems created by the vast numbers of near-Identikit graduates, it would be very simple for the graduate employers to do what they used to do and only look at candidates from the elite universities. A few organizations still do this, but most cannot or at least cannot be seen to be doing too much of it. This is because there exists another and, in this case, contradictory and competing force in modern business. This is the diversity agenda.

The idea that organizations should be diverse is something that has been growing in importance over the last few years. As with so much else in graduate recruitment, the elite employers have led the trend. The Foreign and Commonwealth Office, for example, realized that its white, Oxbridge male image did not sit well with modern Britain under New Labour and moved to change the way it presented itself. At the same time, and with increased investment going into the public sector, the consultancies found themselves bidding against each other for lucrative public-sector contracts which were being awarded by people with a much more interventionist attitude to equal opportunities than they had. In order to win this business they, too, upped their apparent commitment to diversity. Other organizations followed suit, with human resource managers arguing that organizations have to be as multicultural as the community they serve in order to understand their customers and win business. Organizations on a national scale, as most of the graduate recruiters are, therefore need to try to be as multicultural as the whole country. There is no doubt that for this and other business reasons, as well as for deeply held ethical reasons, most human resource managers in graduate recruiting companies are committed to the diversity agenda.

The notion of the war for talent and the diversity agenda are not mutually exclusive. That rare person with talent can come from anywhere. However, when it comes to graduate recruitment this creates a problem. The employers can no longer defeat the logistical nightmare caused by the 20-to-1 ratio by limiting their search to the elite universities, just because students from the minority ethnicities and from the white working class are much less likely to be found there. In theory, therefore, all graduate jobs should be marketed towards, and be open to, all 400,000 graduates.

The interaction between the diversity agenda and the 20-to-1 ratio has placed employers on the horns of a painful dilemma. The war for talent urges them towards the elite universities; the diversity agenda pushes them to be open to all. They end up trying to be exclusive and inclusive at the same time. Understanding how they have tried to solve this problem will give you the key to much of how the marketing of graduate recruitment really works.

Factor four – the knowledge brand

The knowledge brand is fundamental to what recruiters really want from graduates. Like so much else in graduate recruitment, this is another invention of the consultancies. With no actual product to brand and a service which is both difficult to understand and impossible to compare (how do you judge the results of one consultancy's three-year business process re-engineering project against the results its competitors might have had should they have won the bid?), the consultancies had a problem. The knowledge brand is their solution. Instead of suffusing their brand values into inanimate products and marketing messages, they simply branded their employees. Being a successful consultant is all about using body language, demeanour, tone, dress, attitudes and other subtleties of presentation to convey to the client brand qualities such as intellect, compatibility, trustworthiness, integrity, commitment and, above all, expertise. Of course it helps to have the expertise, but what the clients are really buying is a social performance that instils in them complete confidence in the calibre of the performer (and hence the legitimacy of charging whopping great fees). When you are a consultant, the product your clients are buying is you.

> You have to remember that these people are walking into organizations and asking for hundreds of millions of pounds in investment. If they are tongue tied, lack social skills, cannot handle themselves in certain situations, you cannot expect potential clients to be instilled with a degree of confidence in what they are seeing and hearing. You have to have the right kinds of social skills to bring these deals off. *(Consultancy)*

It is this ability to instil confidence in customers, in short to sell the service, that marks out the stars of the modern business world. And where the stars go the others follow. The knowledge brand might not be quite as important to other graduate recruiters as it is to the consultancies – obviously a chemical engineering company is going to want chemists first and brand-embodiers second – but do not be taken in by this. Apart from a very few, highly technical jobs, all employers want people who can manage accounts and generate sales through the embodiment of the organization's values.

Behind all the talk of competencies, all the words about teamworking, communication skills and business awareness, what graduate recruiters want more than anything are graduates who can embody their particular knowledge brand.

Factor five – self-actualization through work

If the knowledge brand is something that works outwards to convince others that you will do a good job, the idea of self-actualization through work is something that goes inwards to convince yourself that you are *in* the right job.

Self-actualization through work is the idea that somewhere out there in the employment universe is a self-shaped hole. If you can find it, it will make you so fulfilled, happy, productive and useful that it hardly matters how much money you make (although the entrepreneurial version of this belief suggests that if you do find that hole you will become rich almost automatically, just because you are good at something). It is a very seductive idea, and is used subtly by employers through-out the recruitment process. For example, it is used both to attract people to the organization – 'working here takes a special type of person' – and to put people off – 'do you really have the commitment and drive needed to succeed in this organization?' It is also used in assessment centres to test how genuine your ambition to work there really is.

The idea of self-actualization through work is attractive, but it is not without its problems. First, like the embodiment of the knowledge brand, it is something that is performed. You might know when you are up for the perfect job for you; the interviewers will not, so you will have to convince them. And you might find yourself up against candidates who suit the job less well but who are better able to be convincing. Indeed, the idea that work should self-actualize you is now so widespread among graduates of all ages that an admission that you are not being self-actualized by your work is tantamount to an admission of failure.

The second problem with the idea of self-actualization through work should be obvious to anyone who has watched 'Pop Idol'. There are more people who want to be stars than there are star-shaped holes. Or to put it another way, there are very very few people who want to self-actualize as dustmen. Or, to bring us back to the beginning of Part 1, there are more aspiring graduates than there are aspirational graduate jobs, by a ratio of 20-to-1.

These, then, are the five factors that have changed graduate recruitment. The rest of this book will show you how you can work these changes to your advantage.

Part

2

Choosing where to apply

2

Choosing where to apply – the facts

The decision about where you apply is obviously one of the most important you can make. It is something over which you should have complete control. Employers, however, do not see it this way. For years now they have been finding techniques for keeping the number of applications they receive to a minimum in terms of quantity and a maximum in terms of quality. They do it in two main ways. They either do not tell you about the jobs if they do not think you will be up to it, or they tell you about them but make you think twice about whether you should send in an application. What the facts section will do is show you the tricks employers use to get inside your head and control what you do. Once you realize the game they are playing, the strategies section will show you what moves you can make in response.

All graduates are not equal. When you hear higher education and employment being discussed, everyone talks as if the world is divided into graduates and non-graduates. It isn't. The world is divided into elite graduates and everyone else (in this context, the only advantage of having a degree is that it is the minimum entry qualification for getting into an elite graduate job). In fact, there is twice as much variation in the salaries of graduates as there is between graduates and non-graduates.

The whole point of this book is to show you how people get selected into the elite; it is not here to maintain the fiction that all graduates have equal opportunities for top employment. However, we do believe that everyone has some sort of chance and that the more you understand how the system really works, the better chance you have. So, in Part 2 we will include some information that is dependent on what sort of university you go to. The reason we are doing it this way is because, when it comes to the marketing of their opportunities, this is exactly how employers behave. We recommend that you read it all because you need to know what advantages and disadvantages the people you are competing against have.

The war for talent versus the diversity agenda

Part 1 showed how employers are caught in the trickiest of situations. The war for talent pushes them towards limiting their graduate hunting to the elite universities, while the diversity agenda shoves them out towards the rank and file. However, there is one further factor to this dynamic, and that is cost. Graduate recruiters cannot afford to visit every university in order to tell all students about their vacancies, nor can they cope with the administrative and procedural burden that the potentially many tens of thousands of applications would create. So, when push meets shove, and they are forced to choose between perceived talent and actual diversity, guess which one loses? Diversity of course.

Cost, then, is the factor that tips the balance and pushes the employers away from the candidates they would encounter at the lower-ranked universities and back towards the talent they think they get from the elite universities. One employer put it like this:

> Oxford and Cambridge still give you overall the best candidates. What it doesn't give you is diversity. And you can't do the two things. *(City bank)*

So they do not. Apart from a few duty visits to lower-ranked universities and to diversity careers fairs, graduate employers mostly piggyback their selection procedures onto those of the top universities and limit their search for the talent of the future to the places they have always looked. This strategy is known as targeting, because employers target their recruitment spend towards those universities where they believe they get the best value for money (i.e. the best candidates). Many of the leading companies will target around 10–15 universities, although this varies.

How targeting works

The higher up the league tables the university, the more likely it is to be targeted by recruiters. This is not a perfect relationship and there are other variables. For instance, no two recruiters will agree on which universities are worth targeting. Some will follow league tables; some will go where they have found good people before; and some will go to those places where they know there are relevant courses. Many recruiters are based in London so, all other things being equal, the further you are from the capital, the less likely they are to pay you a visit. Conversely, lower-ranked universities in the London area do tend to benefit from those diversity-driven duty visits.

All the universities we target, there are very solid reasons for doing it. We use the Times Top 100 to look at the best universities and the best electronic engineering courses. We look at how many graduates they take on each year so we're not targeting a fantastic course that only has three graduates. So that's how we target the 15, but [it's] the same as you would expect: you know Nottingham, Newcastle, Sheffield, Loughborough, Oxford and Cambridge, and Durham. *(Telecoms company)*

We have got some good links now with the University of X, partly because they are local, that is the main thing, it is because they happen to be a local university. Yes, they are one of the top universities but that is almost a bit of the by the way. We send information out to about 100 different universities in terms of a pack to the careers service, then there are 40 universities that are on our higher target list . . . then we go to about 10–12 careers fairs so that is getting it down to the finest point really. *(Car manufacturer)*

The effect of targeting is obvious: the higher up your university is in the league tables, the more top employers you are going to see around campus.

But it is not just about careers fairs and presentations. The employers also use other methods to control the amount of information you receive about their opportunities. For example, they can use a third party to do their contacting work for them. There are a number of services that operate to limit the number of students who are told about an employer's graduate training scheme. There are marketing organizations that employ student brand managers to spread the word about opportunities, and there are even headhunters who use student leaders (society presidents and the like) to suggest likely candidates (themselves and their friends) to the company. However, the most widely used method of third-party targeting is through one of the graduate recruitment websites. If you are at a top university, you will have been approached many times to sign up to them. They work by collecting details of tens of thousands of students and graduates and then selling the facility to search the database to employers. The employers are then able to pick out a carefully defined group (selected by degree subject *and* university *and* A-level results, for example). They then email this targeted group either with news of opportunities and application deadlines, or with invitations to exclusive on-campus events.

The pros of being at a heavily targeted university

You might think that the great advantage to being at a highly targeted university is all the information you receive about what opportunities are available. However, the real benefit is not in learning about opportunities; the benefit comes from all the insider tips you are able to glean about the recruitment process.

Careers fairs and presentations give you the opportunity to observe and talk to company representatives. Anyone can look through a company website, but we all know that there is nothing more truly interactive than another human being. This person can give you direct hints on success, explain problems with the application form; they may even, if they like you, give you their card and suggest you contact them if you have any further questions during the application process. This is such valuable information that it almost amounts to insider trading.

Second, you can make decisions in context about how that organization presents itself in comparison with other organizations at the fair. You can, for example, get a feel for the market by seeing how popular a stand is in comparison with others.

But there is a further, much more subtle and important advantage of being able to see employers face to face. This comes from what it enables you to learn about their knowledge brand. All but the most inexperienced graduate recruiters understand the need to present themselves to students in a strategic manner. And to this end they have developed a younger, funkier version of their knowledge brand known as the graduate brand.

Among these employers, everything that you see at a presentation or at a careers fair has been thought through in terms of its branding: the people chosen to staff the stand, the ties or skirts they wear (they don't have to be told: they *know*), the backdrop, the literature or DVDs they hand out, the sweets and the drinks they give away. All this provides you with very good information on precisely the qualities they want you to embody as an applicant.

You can process this information both consciously and unconsciously. Looking at the stands and talking to the people on them, you can work out how they dress and how they present themselves and make a judgement about whether you share these characteristics or whether you can present yourself in the same way. Or you can simply decide whether you feel comfortable and enthusiastic about applying to that organization.

In short, all of this helps you make judgements about where you might apply to and what you will need to include in the application in order to succeed. Students attending careers fairs which attract top organizations are able to make highly informed decisions about where they should apply. This gives them an advantage over people who go to not such well-attended fairs who have to make less well-informed, more speculative applications.

The cons of being at a heavily targeted university

However, even if you are at a top university, you do not have it all your own way. The single biggest personal danger you face is developing an arrogant and complacent attitude. You see employers going to such efforts to come to your university and present themselves to you in an attractive way, and you assume that you are a valuable commodity and that employers are fighting among themselves to attract you to their organization. This is a natural conclusion to come to and it is completely inaccurate.

First, there really are not enough jobs to justify this attitude whichever university you go to. According to the Chief Executive of the Association of Graduate Recruiters, the last time graduates really had the upper hand over employers was in about 1990. In the meantime, the graduate glut has gone on growing and the number of AGR jobs does not now even add up to the number of undergraduates at the University of Salford. Second, the marketing of opportunities can often have more to do with developing the reputation of the knowledge brand than it has to do with the mechanics of finding new employees. Remember how in Part 1 we hinted that an elite reputation in the graduate marketplace enhanced the reputations of those already in an organization? The same is true of the organization itself. Some companies with relatively few vacancies are happy to present themselves to very large numbers of graduates at the top universities in order to enhance their reputations among the future managerial elite. International consulting companies, for example, make their money by persuading other organizations that only they have the skills to implement some development. The people who make these decisions are almost always people who themselves have joined graduate training programmes so an elite graduate brand is a way of marketing the consultancy's services to its future customers.

What all this means for you is that it is very easy to overestimate the number of jobs on offer. In fact, there is no relationship between the marketing an organization does and the number of vacancies it has. This is how one expert on the graduate market puts it:

> You can't really draw any conclusions about how many vacancies an employer has from the extent of its on-campus activities. Some employers might visit 25 universities and do 3 presentations at each, attracting audiences of 150 students a time. However, they might only have 60 vacancies, so their on-campus activity could seem out of proportion to their needs . . . In short, there is no correlation between the extent of an organization's profile on campus and the number of vacancies it has available. The only conclusion that a student can draw from the presence of companies on campus is that his or her university is considered an important source of employees for those companies. (Leading graduate opinion pollster)

The upshot of this is that if you go to an elite university it is possible that you will end up applying to an organization where you have a far worse chance of getting a job than the 20-to-1 ratio we explored in Part 1. Despite their targeting efforts, some elite graduate recruiters report ratios between applications and vacancies of upwards of 40-to-1. This might seem to undermine all their targeting efforts, but it is probable that they are prepared to tolerate the administrative burden of sifting through these applications because of the image it gives them.

There are, however, points in the recruitment and economic cycle when employers start to tolerate even higher ratios: from several hundreds to one to perhaps even thousands to one.

This happens when employers either continue to market vacancies aggressively when their vacancy numbers have been cut or opt to maintain their presence in the graduate market when they have absolutely no need from a recruitment point of view to do so. Both these situations occur because building a graduate brand is expensive and the collective student memory is very short. With the student population churning by a third each year, graduate recruiters have to protect their initial investment by maintaining their brand presence year in year out, even when their recruitment needs are changing. Graduate campaigns are planned up to a year in advance, while business needs and decisions can be much more short term. There are times, therefore, when recruiters find they have filled their vacancies for the year, but still have fairs left to do. The trouble is that withdrawing from the market for even a single year can seriously damage perception of the graduate brand and of the organization as a regular graduate recruiter, while admitting to a mid-year cut in vacancies does not give anyone the best impression. While some companies react to this problem by cutting back their recruitment activities proportionately or by abandoning them altogether, a few may elect to carry on as if nothing has happened.

Autumn campaigns are organized in the spring, and if in the meantime economic conditions change and they find they need fewer graduates than they originally thought, a company might opt to continue with the campaign rather than pay the cancellation charges for fairs and presentations it has already got in place. *(Leading graduate opinion pollster)*

This overall cut in vacancies can be significant. In 2001–2, the AGR's figures suggest that as many as 2,700 graduate vacancies disappeared during the course of the year (or more than 15 percent of the total number that companies had originally anticipated recruiting). Many organizations may have been quite open about this, but it does appear that some AGR companies neglected to reveal that they were not taking as many graduates as they had originally stated.

'Anecdotal evidence from individual recruiters confirms that during the 2001–2 recruiting season many employers continued to promote vacancy levels that were similar to the previous year,' says the AGR's report on that year, 'but at the end of the year quietly elected not to fill all their places, rather than publicly declare a cut in vacancies.'

The implication of much of the above is that graduate recruiters are quite prepared to encourage students to apply for jobs that may not exist in any real sense. However, there is no direct proof of this. What we can confidently assert is that some companies opt to stay in the graduate market just to keep the graduate brand going. They may, for example, advertise themselves through one of the online databases when in fact they only have a single vacancy and could certainly fill it in other ways. This is not about recruitment but about marketing, and in some cases the ratio of applications to places could easily be several hundreds to one.

The pros and cons of being at a less well-targeted university

You will have probably worked out that the pros and cons of being at a lower-ranked university are the opposite of being at somewhere highly targeted. On the one hand you don't get all that free information about what sort of people the companies are looking for. This is a major disadvantage, but it is *only* information, and you should be able to find it in other ways. Your other major disadvantage is, of course, the use of A-level grades as a pre-set deselection criterion, but we shall come to this in a moment. On the other hand, one advantage you do have is that you are not going to be misled by the marketing to assume there are more jobs on offer than there are. You know it is going to be difficult to get an aspirational job, so, unlike your peers at the big-name universities, you are not going to miss out on a graduate job because of arrogance or complacency. Being realistic is always an advantage.

The second trick: self-selection

Apart from not telling vast swathes of graduates about their vacancies, graduate recruiters have a second trick they use to cut down on applications. They make you think you are not right for the job and get you to abandon the idea of making an application altogether. This technique is called self-selection and it succeeds by bringing into play the idea of self-actualization through work.

As we saw in Part 1, self-actualization through work is a very seductive concept. We all want to believe that we are unique individuals with a blend of skills, attributes and experiences that make us ideally suited to a specific career. We want to believe it, but it's probably not true. A generation or two ago the whole idea would have been seen as ridiculously self-indulgent; back then, fulfilment came from doing a job as well as you could and in being useful to society. Today, however, self-actualization through work is so ubiquitously approved of that you probably have not given it a second thought.

In graduate recruitment you are going to come up against two versions of the self-actualization belief: the weak, official version and the strong, marketing version. The weak, official version is propounded by advice organs such as the careers service and is something which nobody could reasonably object to. This version argues that before you start applying you should take stock of who you are, look at the experiences you have enjoyed, and base your job-hunting strategies on what all this tells you about yourself.

The strong, marketing version takes this reasonable and liberating approach and turns it into a deselection tool. The Royal Marines' slogan is the perfect example. The words '99.9% *need not apply*' force every potential applicant to consider very seriously his or her suitability for the role. It functions to maintain the elite image of the organization while simultaneously preventing too many wannabes swamping its recruitment function with applications, much like a good graduate recruitment campaign aims to do. However, while most people would be prepared to accept that only one in a thousand of us might have the capabilities to become a Royal Marine, it is more difficult to believe that the requirements for becoming a successful information technology (IT) consultant are similarly rigorous. That, of course, does not stop the graduate recruitment marketers from attempting to make the same claim. It is important, therefore, to be aware that too much emphasis on self-actualization and self-selection can easily be turned into a form of deselection by self. And deselecting yourself from any position that you might reasonably be able to get is a poor strategy.

The final technique: minimum qualifications (the UCAS points bar)

The final technique employers can use to control the number of applications they receive is to specify minimum academic qualifications. This is both a marketing technique (because it stops some candidates from ever applying) and what is known as a sifting technique (because it is a way of sending large proportions of candidates who do apply through the hole marked rejection).

The main justification employers have for using UCAS points as a form of self-selection/deselection is that they see them as a way of predicting future performance. Accountancy firms particularly point to a correlation between A-level grades and the ability to pass professional examinations, and use them to avoid the costs of employing candidates who are at a greater risk of failing their exams. The reasons for this correlation are unclear, but it may be that both A-levels and accountancy exams require the ability to cover several subjects at once.

It is worth pointing out that this may be a practice that becomes harder to justify after the adoption of European age legislation (because mature students are less likely to have A-levels and certainly less likely to have benefited from the grade-inflation towards straight As of the last few years). However, whatever the justification for using A-level grades, as you might guess, the real reason for using them is that they are a fantastically cheap and easy means of getting rid of huge numbers of potential and actual applicants. Because of this, around a half of all graduate recruiters use them in some way. There is, however, a lot of variation in how they are used between industries and between employers. First, the less an organization relies on professional qualifications, the less likely it is to specify a minimum UCAS requirement. Second, while some might use them as an automatic bar, many other recruiters see them as being just one factor among many. They score application forms according to a range of pre-determined criteria (which might even include GCSEs) and it is the total that matters. If the academic points are not high, the deficit can therefore be made up elsewhere.

We don't say you have to have a minimum UCAS points because some people can do great in the GCSEs, but when it comes to the A-levels have a really bad time, then go to a university that maybe they wouldn't have chosen to go to ultimately. But they messed up their A-levels and come out with a First at that university. They are a bright, well-rounded person, who we could have missed because we say 'Oh they went to this university', or, 'They only have this many UCAS points so why should we look at them?' and we could have missed our star . . . We have a minimum of a 2.2 in a logical or numerate discipline but we don't like to be too rigid. We don't want the 'Stepford Wives' robot systems. Somebody can redeem themselves in the last paragraph and look pretty good. *(IT consultancy)*

What we do is we try and encourage candidates to screen themselves out. We're up front about our criteria. It's all very well putting it on the website that we do this so, when we go through the applications, on the first page, you actually fill out by clicking yes or no [to these questions]. Do you have the right number of UCAS points? Are you expecting a 2.1? Have you got the right to work in the UK? Are you fluent in English? Have you graduated less than two years ago? And if you click no, you can still apply through extenuating circumstances, but it will point them through to our careers website as well. There are some graduates going through even though they don't meet the criteria. What we will look at when we screen them is, do they meet the basic criteria? If they don't, are there extenuating circumstances? *(Telecoms company)*

We try and be flexible in that we advertise 22 UCAS points and a 2.1. However, because of equality and diversity and being fair to the candidates and how we assess them at first round, we are not sticking rigidly to that ... If they completed a really strong application form, answered the questions really well, we would say, 'yes, 18, not too bad, really good application form, they've obviously got something about them here', then we would still put them through ... We offer a variation of grey in the middle ... [However] I think that's where it will change for next year ... I think we will have to stick to the 22 UCAS points and be more rigorous and maybe more ruthless around the entry requirement. Because if we're going to be looking for less, and we are wanting the best, then why are we wavering and doing what we do? Although we're trying to do the right thing by the candidates. *(High street bank)*

Students at lower-ranked universities and the double whammy

It is worth saying at this point that we have never heard of any employer using any sort of scoring system for universities, that is we have never heard of anyone systematically rejecting people because they went to the wrong type of university. Obviously this may happen, and individual recruitment personnel may have their own prejudices, but, if it goes beyond this, the employers are keeping very quiet about it.

However, there is no doubt that targeting and the UCAS points bar have almost the same effect as selection based on university, and this creates something of a double whammy for students of lower-ranked universities. Not only do employers not tell you about their vacancies, if by some chance you get to hear about them, they stop you from successfully applying anyway.

Talking to employers, you can get the impression they are a little embarrassed by this. They know very well that it is bad for the diversity agenda they espouse. They know that it undermines the grandeur of their war for talent, turning an epic battle between elite employers fought across every section of society into something that is more like a local scuffle for the good opinion of the posh. They also know that it destroys the (to them still useful) division between graduates and non-graduates. They do, after all, present themselves as *graduate* recruiters, not *people-with-good-A-levels-who-go-to-elite-universities* recruiters. This is important, and it may be that employers understand that when government policy is committed to sending half of all young people to university it is in their best interests to maintain the fiction that a degree from one university is just as acceptable to them as a degree from any other. However, what it means, if you are a student at a lower-ranked university, is that you are still in with a chance. In fact, the diversity agenda may even give you a subtle advantage over some of your peers at the higher-ranked institutions.

The diversity agenda may be quite a weak force in graduate recruitment. But this does not mean it does not exist. One graduate recruitment manager put it like this:

We've just got a diversity sponsor . . . because we're . . . quite young, it's a bit sophisticated for us. With graduate recruitment, [diversity] is not something we discourage but not something we actively encourage. So it's difficult because with some things like the brochure . . . I'm always conscious that it is slightly staged. I make sure we have a cross-section of representatives so it can be anything from having a white engineer but doing yoga, which is challenging the stereotypes, to making sure we have a female Asian person in our adverts and a male Asian person in our adverts and in our brochure. But it is not something we are actively doing at the moment, actively targeting . . . like I say it is quite unsophisticated . . . I mean the fact that it's on the web is going to increase diversity. *(Telecoms company)*

As this graduate recruitment manager knows, just hoping that people from non-traditional backgrounds and lower-ranked universities are going to stumble across a website is not the most proactive diversity strategy. Good intentions are easily overwhelmed by cost issues created by the graduate glut and the importance attached to the war for talent. Yet, however ineffectual their efforts to lead their organization towards greater diversity, the graduate recruitment departments (not the most powerful branch of elite organizations) do believe in it and try their best.

What this does mean is that they would love to get some suitable candidates from outside the elite universities. A

good-quality application from a low-ranked university therefore makes them happy. It affirms them in their commitment
to diversity; it shows them that their marketing and recruitment strategies can unearth talent wherever it comes from;
and it confirms them in their belief that the war for talent is
about creating a managerial meritocracy rather than something which merely serves to solidify class advantages. They
like that.

CHAPTER 3

Choosing where to apply – the strategies

Graduate recruitment is all about selecting the best candidates. In theory, the best are selected at every stage: at the assessment centre, after the first interview, after the online tests, and after the application form. But there is one stage prior to the application form that is easy to miss. This is what might be called pre-selection by marketing, and its effect is to deselect vast numbers of students and graduates before the application procedure has even begun. The facts section showed how employers have two ways to stop you applying. The first is simple: they do not tell you about the jobs. The second is more subtle: they make you think that the job is not for you or use A-level grades to stop you applying. At the same time they can mislead you into thinking there are more opportunities than there really are. Here are the five key strategies you must use if you are to counteract the employers' marketing tricks and techniques.

Strategy one – apply to as many employers as you possibly can

The recruitment industry will hate this piece of advice because it short-circuits all its efforts to restrict applicant numbers. Nevertheless, it should be obvious that the more quality, researched and targeted applications you make, the better your chances will be of getting an aspirational graduate job.

It is easy to forget this, however, because of the way the recruitment industry plays upon the idea of self-actualization through work (see Chapter 1). There is of course nothing wrong with the idea that you should seek out work that you will be good at and which you will enjoy. It would be absurd to say otherwise. However, this does not mean that you should only have a single employment goal. Like the vast majority of people, there will be a number of very different jobs you could do equally well, and the strategy of limiting yourself to one career goal is therefore a poor one (because there will always be far fewer aspirational jobs than there are people who are suited to them). Remember that you have the rest of your life to change your career direction but that you can only get one first job. If you want to join the elite, you are much better off getting into any elite employment at this stage and moving around than you are waiting for what you perceive to be the perfect job to come along.

You should, therefore, ignore the general blandishments of the recruitment industry to send out only a very few applications to your ideal jobs. You should also ignore the subtle self-actualization techniques employers use to make you think that their job is not for you. They are not trying to limit applications for your benefit but for their own. In terms of the mechanics of getting an aspirational graduate job, you are much better off applying to a large number of employers, aiming at a number of different employment goals, and moving between a range of industries and sectors.

Strategy two – use your careers service to find out about less popular employers

It is very easy to go to a careers fair or put your details on a graduate recruitment website. However, if you only do this you will be limiting the information you have to quite a small number of employers and, although they might seem to have plenty of jobs (why else would they be there?), this should never be taken for granted.

As we saw in the facts section, the amount of marketing an employer does can give a misleading impression of the number of vacancies they actually have available. Some of them pull in thousands and thousands of applications while only having a few dozen vacancies to fill. This can create ratios of applicants to vacancies of well over 40-to-1. You should, therefore, play them at their own game and make sure you target some of your applications to those less popular employers where you have a better chance of success.

In order to do this you will need to visit your careers service. The employers do not have your interests at heart, the careers service does. It has information on hundreds of potential employers, it is free and the advisors will have a great knowledge of the market. They will also have contacts in graduate recruitment companies whom they can exploit. You can use the service up to several years after graduation and you will usually be able to use another university's, if it is closer to where you live (sometimes for a small fee). True, it is not glamorous, it may be full of people who are shielded from the realities of a competitive job market, they may push the self-actualization line too hard and discourage some of the strategies we will show you, but it is the single most useful resource that you will ever have for job hunting.

By going to your careers service, you will be able to find out about organizations that are recruiting but which hardly market themselves at all and so have much lower, much more applicant-friendly ratios.

In order to get some purchase on what the actual ratio might be, you first need to find out how many vacancies they have. Some employers will give this vacancy information on their website. If they do not, you could ring and ask. They may say they cannot be specific; if they say this, you should ask whether it is a handful, a few dozen, or over a hundred. If they still will not say, it is worth asking a careers advisor for an educated guess. Information on the number of applications can be harder to come by. Again, you can ask for a ballpark figure and if they do not respond you can ask a careers service advisor for his or her opinion.

Strategy three – be systematic in your approach

None of the above means that we are advocating a scattergun approach in which you fire off hundreds of more or less identical applications in all directions. Remember that it is *quality*, *researched* and *targeted* applications that should be maximized. In the next section we will show you how to create these successful applications and why they work, but you should know now that sending out low-quality, under-researched, scattergun applications will not.

Creating these quality applications takes time, and your time is valuable. All graduates have economic pressures to contend with, while final-year students have academic pressures as well. You should, therefore, decide how many applications you can reasonably make per week and then keep to it. Next, create a to-do list of potential employers, mix them up so you are applying for more than one career goal and also to unpopular employers, and work through the pile until you are either offered a job or you have enough information to decide why you are not being offered one (if this is happening to you, you should see Part 5).

Strategy four – use on-campus events to study the knowledge brand

Instead of seeing careers fairs and other on-campus events as places in which you are given information about vacancies and working conditions, you should try to see careers fairs and the like as an opportunity to gain information about the knowledge brand. You need to look at the people staffing the stand and ask yourself what sort of people this organization is looking for. Also, should you make a connection with one of them, you might, if you make the right impression, even make a contact who is prepared to give you some inside tips on the recruitment process.

If you are at a lower-ranked university and you find that not enough of the employers you are interested in are coming to your careers fair, it is worth trying to get into one that they *are* going to visit. A lot of cities have two universities and the careers department at the more prestigious one will try to stop students from the less prestigious university going to its career fairs (they have to maintain the purity of their candidate pool in order to attract the elite employers in the first place). This is not high security however and it is usually possible to gain entry.

Strategy five – never apply without the minimum qualification, unless . . .

The one thing you should never do is send applications to employers when you do not have the minimum academic qualification they require. It will be wasted effort as you will be automatically deselected. If you believe there will be a problem with your qualifications the best thing you can do is find out as much as possible about the way a company scores the application form. If you find that you will be automatically deselected because you do not have the right A-levels, degree result or degree subject, you have only one choice.

The only way round this is if you can find somebody in the organization who is prepared to look at your application regardless. You either have to go to a careers fair and make your case in person, or you have to do it on the phone (or in some cases present your extenuating circumstances on an online form). In order to do any of these you will have to be as well prepared as you would be if you were about to step into an assessment centre, so you should read the rest of this book first.

Choosing where to apply – the tactics

Once you start looking, you will find you come across opportunities very quickly and it can sometimes be difficult to decide whether or not each one is worth pursuing. You should, therefore, ask yourself these five quick tactical questions and only decide to put an opportunity on your application to-do list if you can answer yes to all of them.

Do I have the minimum academic qualification they require?

If not, do not apply by the normal route because you will be automatically deselected; you must find a different way in.

Does this job fit my applications strategy?

To maximize your chances you need to apply to a strategic range of employers: a mix of big names and small names, popular and unpopular, primary and secondary career goals. However, this does not mean that you should apply everywhere. Creating quality applications takes time and, although you should never cut and paste, by concentrating on only two or three specific industries you will become more experienced at completing each style of application form. If you are endlessly jumping between different types of industry this benefit will be lost. So, if it does not fit in, ignore this one for the moment and find another prospective employer.

Can I do this job?

This goes beyond minimum qualifications and into the area of deselection by self (and remember that employers encourage this). So, it might not be your dream job, but ask yourself whether you would be good at it anyway.

Is this job good enough – do I want it enough to put in the time and effort involved in making a quality application?

As we said above and as you will see in the next chapter, there is no point making poor-quality applications. Employers easily spot them and throw them out.

Am I like the graduates in this employer's brochure, or who come to their presentations, or staff their career stands, or can I be like them?

Employers show you precisely the kinds of people they are looking for in the brochures and at on-campus events. These are people who embody their graduate brand. Despite any claim the organization might make about encouraging diversity, if you are not like them already, or do not want to be like them, or are not prepared to be like them, you are not likely to get through the assessment centre stage. So, if the answer is no, ignore this one and find another prospective employer.

Part

3

What to put on application forms

CHAPTER 5

What to put on application forms – the facts

On the basis of four to five thousand applications, we very easily get what we're looking for. I'm not so sure there's a war . . . for talent . . . at this stage, it's more a war of turning them away. *(High street bank)*

Once upon a time, being a graduate was almost enough to get you an interview on its own. Employers knew that this made you part of a small, highly educated elite. They knew that this not only gave you the intellectual skills to cope with complex professional and managerial tasks, it also gave you a natural authority that caused people to listen to what you had to say and look up to you. Recruitment was just a quick glance through your CV to check the specifics of your intellectual accomplishments followed by an interview to make sure that you were the sort of person your superiors would enjoy spending time with.

But the number of graduates began to grow, grants disappeared and loans increased and many more people were now graduates, with many of them also having work experience to include on their CVs. Now it was not enough for candidates only to be academically able. Employers realized that they could choose between you by looking beyond your educational achievements and examining what you got up to outside the library and the lecture hall. If they looked at your application and saw that you were the sort of person who could pull off a 2.1 while simultaneously working *and* leading a rich extra-curricula life, they assumed that you had more to offer them than someone who had only gone to university and got a degree. So this became the basis on which they picked candidates for interview.

But the number of graduates continued to grow. Now there were so many different CVs with so many different types of experience that employers found it harder to justify choosing one type of apparent evidence of skills over another. Was it better to be football captain and to have worked in a pizza parlour? Or to be a debating captain and to have volunteered to help sort contributions for famine relief? So employers tried to stop making assumptions from your non-academic experience about what skills you had. At the same time, employers started to define the skills, competencies and aptitudes they felt were particularly important in their industry and organization, and then to ask for candidates to show evidence of these. They started to want graduates who showed that they understood that qualifications and extra-curricular activities were not an end in themselves but merely a means of developing these skills, competencies and attributes that employers wanted to see. Now the people who were picked for interview had to be people who could see their skills development from the employer's point of view.

And this is how we got where we are today.

WHAT ARE SKILLS, COMPETENCIES AND APTITUDES?

All these words mean more or less the same thing. They are the abilities that are required to do the job on offer. About a decade ago, organizations began to try to make their selection procedures more rigorous. One of the ways they did this was to make the selection criteria more explicit. Instead of picking people on the basis of the interviewer's instinct and assumption, they tried to define what skills were needed to successfully do the job. In graduate recruitment, they would often do this by examining the skills that senior managers in the organization had and then looking for evidence of these skills in the candidates. For instance, although it is obvious that to be good at IT you need to be numerate, the people who really succeed in IT organizations are those who are good team players (among other things). IT companies, therefore, began to ask for evidence of team working from their candidates.

The current NHS graduate programme (**www.future leaders.nhs.uk**) provides a typical example of what employers are looking for. There are eight competencies required for this programme and they are divided into three broad areas.

People:

- leading and taking responsibility
- communicating and influencing
- working with others.

▶

Task:

- driving for and achieving results
- managing, planning and organizing.

Thinking:

- analytical thinking
- numerical ability
- broad-based problem solving and decision making.

Although competencies are supposed to be organization and industry specific, the fact is that most graduate recruiters are looking for more or less the same things (although they may call them by different names). What they all want are candidates with people skills (team working, the ability to influence others, etc.), leadership potential (project management, decisiveness, the drive to succeed, etc.), and relevant technical ability (numeracy, problem-solving skills, etc.). Then there is business awareness. This is an increasingly important competency in the private sector and it comes down to realizing that all business activity is geared towards making a profit (the equivalent competency in the public sector is organizational awareness). What makes the system confusing is that different organizations divide up the competencies in different ways and give them slightly different names.

This, of course, is one of the holes in the competency-based system. No two recruiters (or their consultants) will agree on exactly how to define, for example, the drive to succeed. A second problem is the way the competencies bleed into one another. One company's evidence of good team working is another's evidence of communication skills, while one's example of decision making is another assessor's evidence of leadership potential. Finally, as we will see in Part 4, the biggest problem with competencies is that so many of them are the difficult-to-measure soft skills (hard skills are things such as numeracy, which can be objectively tested, while soft skills are abilities such as team working, which are very much in the eye of the beholder).

The great advantage of the competency-based system for you, however, is the way that it makes organizations be very clear about exactly what it is they want to see from you. All you have to do is read the website thoroughly, appreciate what competencies they wish to see evidence of, and then provide this by answering the questions properly.

What employers want

Like any good story, some of the above is an over-simplification, but what this potted history of graduate recruitment shows is this. Employers want to see five things on an application form (which, like a child's development in the womb, mimic the stages in the evolutionary history of graduate recruitment over the last 20 years).

1. Academic/technical qualifications

There are a few jobs where you can lock them in a cupboard, shove them a cord and bring it out at the end, but not that many. *(IT consultancy)*

At the very simplest level, they want to know that you have the hard academic and technical skills required for the job. For some jobs this will be any degree, for others it will be a degree in a subject area (a numerate degree, for example), and occasionally it might be a degree in a specific subject. They will also usually require GCSEs in perhaps maths and English and (in many cases) a specified number of UCAS points. This, of course, is the minimum level of qualification. It is unlikely that there are any graduates left who still think that having the minimum qualifications will get them an interview. In fact, it is not even worth applying, if this is all you have. (Having said this, however, there are a very few, highly specialized jobs where the pool of candidates with the minimum qualification is so small that you might just get through without any other attributes, although in these cases the minimum qualification is more likely to be a PhD than a first degree.)

2. Extra-curricular activities

What I say to people is that most of the people on the short list have already got the academics. They have got 22 UCAS points so you are all the same, so this is where you stand out. So if you say 'I have a degree, I have three As at A-level and I have passed my driving test', you are not really that interesting and you haven't really stood out. *(Accountancy firm)*

The ones that [succeed] have got off their backsides and done something a bit different. Who have done their gap year, who have done Raleigh [International], who've had lots of different work experience and not necessarily paid, who have done a bit of voluntary work, who have done the Duke of Edinburgh's even, although some of them are a bit geeky. *(Telecoms company)*

To stand any sort of chance you must also have some extra-curricular activities (work, travel, volunteering, social, sporting, and club or society membership, etc.). Effectively what these activities do is give you the resources to take part in the real competition. Having a good range of extra-curricular experiences does, however, bring you a lot further than merely having the minimum academic or technical qualification. There are still a few otherwise professional organizations that continue to recruit on the basis of inferences made about who you are from your qualifications *and* the type of non-academic achievements you have – small accountancy firms, for example (the one quoted above is actually quite large). These more old-fashioned employers will not be real players in the graduate market, except perhaps at their local universities.

3. Awareness that technical/academic qualifications and extra-curricular activities are a means to an end

What we're talking about is giving people the opportunity to illustrate the value of their experiences and to interpret them in different ways. It's really about how they have learned [from the experiences they have had] and how they are able to reflect on their learning. Are they reflective learners?

The kind of candidates that are successful with us, and I think that a lot of other recruiters would agree, is the sort of person that can illustrate [what we are looking for] in their application and articulate that at interview but won't be carrying round a whopping great folder saying 'look, here's my record of achievement'. If they haven't got to the stage where they can write and talk about it in a confident manner, clearly understanding what it means, then it hasn't been of any benefit.
(Consultancy)

This is where you start to get into the game. In the personal statement section of the application form, employers invite you to make the link between what you have done in your life and the skills, competencies and aptitudes (see box on pages 47–49) they need.

They are not looking for you to merely answer these make-or-break questions. They are looking to you to show how seriously you understand the importance of the competency they are eliciting. The personal statement section is, therefore, more than an opportunity to show the skills they are looking for, it is also an opportunity to show you understand the centrality of the notion of being competent in that particular skill.

4. The oomph factor: select and integrate

We look for . . . people who really present themselves well on the application so have a knowledge of all this IT stuff, but you can get a technical application that is just a list of jargon. So they have to come across well and they have to be able to demonstrate to us that they understand what they are doing and it is not technology just for technology's sake, it is technology in order to solve a problem so they have to be very specific because they have to be able to sell their skills in the context of, you know, the application of them. *(IT consultancy)*

If you have achieved all of the above, you have an application and a chance of being put through to the next stage. However, what really takes your application up to another level is if you are able to select and integrate all of the above. The key words here are *select* and *integrate*. Once you have got past the initial sift, employers will take it for granted that you will have the minimum technical/academic requirements for the job. They will also take it for granted that you will have various non-academic, extra-curricular experiences that will have given you opportunities to develop other skills. Of course they still want to see these experiences on your application form, but more than this what they want you to do is *select* the most relevant of them and *integrate* them with the skills, aptitudes or competencies that they tell you they want. It is your job to do this. Employers try not to make too many inferences any more (it feels too subjective and irrational in the age of competency-based recruitment) and why should they? With so many candidates to choose from they can afford to be picky and only take candidates further who demonstrate that they understand that all their experiences, academic and non-academic, were not an end in themselves but a preparation for the specifics of this employment.

If you can do everything so far, your application is starting to look like a dead cert. However, there is an even higher level.

5. Embody the knowledge brand

If you can also suffuse your application with the awareness of the knowledge brand (the organization's values), you have got to the stage where your application has the best chance of success. This is a higher level of integration because it concerns embodying qualities rather than simply providing evidence of competencies. Some employers can be very upfront about what they are looking for. Barclays Bank, for example, is looking for individuals who possess what it calls the 'three Es': people who are 'Exceptional, who demonstrate Edge and who are Energizing in all that they do'. The bank defines people who are 'energizing' in the following way:

They'll . . . be an individual who focuses on the true priorities and achieves great results by overcoming every challenge and obstacle that confronts them. Indeed, their unbridled passion and commitment inspires and motivates others to achieve great things too. They'll be inspirational to those that work with them, communicating at every level in the business with the same enthusiasm to gain support for new ideas and solutions. They will be able to overcome resistance and barriers, focusing on the important issues, to truly make the impossible possible and achieve great business results. (Barclays Bank)

What not to say on application forms

Employers today are therefore very open about what they are looking for in a successful application. They are also very clear about what they do not want to see. The candidates who fail are the ones who do not provide credible evidence that they have the competencies the employers require.

At the moment we've got two, not killer questions, but really good questions that we change from season to season. One talks about your key achievements and the other one talks about a situation that you've had influence over. So what was the situation, what did you do, what was the outcome? There are huge differences . . . in how they answer those two questions . . . We've got criteria that we stick to on how we rate the form but these two questions do start to separate them.

A weak answer is sometimes as simple as whether or not they have read the question. Because they don't read the questions and answer them, they don't give you the answer that you want from them, but very loose or light answers. [For example] 'I was working in my part-time job in Pizza Hut and we had no way of seeing who our customers were, so I came up with the idea and created a database and put everything onto a database and there we are.' That's situation, action and outcome, [but] it's really [too] light . . . Or we have, serious[ly], ones where they will say 'the house that we are all living in as students is really messy and nobody would wash up. I therefore created a rota to wash up and I also laminated this. Outcome, we now get the dishes washed up.'

[A good answer would be] something where they've provided a good situation based on their work experience or something at university, because we ask them obviously for positions of responsibility that they have held, so netball captain, you led the treasury for the club at university, so the example links back to those positions of responsibility and gives a really good situation where they saw something . . . [where] there was a benefit for them that was tangible and they will tell you what that tangible benefit was. It was in savings, it either saved cus-tomers, or it saved money. Something that was quite robust.
(High street bank)

One of the questions on the application form is about working within groups of people and when I first joined university and I was given this project with these people who I had never met, and then you get the next bit. So they all write about [university project work] . . . you keep reading the same thing time and time again . . . half the groups then say, 'oh well I was put with these people that I didn't know and we had to do this presenta-tion together and we decided that because we all had different timetables, we split the work into four sections and we each did our own section and then presented it together at the end'.

▶

They completely missed the point of how did you manage to work with those people and they say 'well we just split it up' and that happens so much on the forms . . . you cringe. *[Car manufacturer]*

What to put on application forms – the strategies

Employers tell you the minimum criteria, they tell you what competencies they wish to see, many of them will also tell you what broader brand attributes they expect, while some of them will even give you model answers. With all this information out there, you would have thought that they should be getting perfect applications. The reason they do not is because they can rely upon the vast majority of candidates to underestimate how much work should go into an application. So, if you put the effort in, if you do the research, study the website and brochure, familiarize yourself with the competencies and the brand values required, and then answer the questions credibly, you will give yourself a much better chance of making it to the next stage.

The strategies section takes you through the key things you must and must not do when putting together an application. As we said in the 'Introduction', there is no point in our providing set answers. They will be copied instantly and so become immediately useless (and it also goes against one of our key strategies – originality). What we do here is provide a series of principles you can use to tailor your experience to the specifics of the organization's requirements.

Strategy one – create each application from scratch

This is essential and very easy not to do. Obviously, your bio details are always going to be the same, but once you have written one or two application forms it is very tempting to cut and paste whole answers from one personal statement section into another one. Do not. Employers can usually spot when you are answering a subtly different question to the one they have posed and, even when the question is identical, the context will be different. No two organizations want the same set of qualifications, skills and knowledge brand. Of course, you might use the same phrases on the two forms, even the same incidents, but because the context will be subtly different so should your answers be.

One of the most important things to realize is that recruiters are after people who genuinely want to work for them and not those who simply want a generic aspirational job. Of course, many of the applications they receive will be from people who want any job, but that just makes them work harder trying to spot a genuinely motivated application (the one that has had time spent on it) from one that has been copied from elsewhere. Occasionally they might make a mistake, and this is why application forms that have been copied from others do sometimes get through. This, however, is a poor strategy because it relies on someone else being incompetent. Generally recruiters are quite good at spotting the stitches that reveal an application has been patched together. They keep a very close eye on what their competitors are doing and sometimes amuse themselves by trying to work out which of their rivals you have applied to previously. Every application form must, therefore, be written from scratch to maximize its chances of success.

Strategy two – the magic formula: create a life story for every individual employer

Creating applications from scratch should go deeper than the simple avoidance of copying. Each application should be unique and tailored to the specifics of the employer's stated requirements. One of the most powerful ways you can do this is to think about what you are doing as creating what we call a narrative of employability. This is a story about yourself which has been created to demonstrate the things an individual employer is looking for. Instead of simply listing all your attributes and experiences, and hoping that the employer will somehow be able to 'read' the evidence that demonstrates you have the attributes they need, what you do is select from all the experiences you have had only those ones that are relevant to this employer. In this way, you create a story of yourself that has a hero (you) with estimable qualities (a combination of technical/academic skills and character-based competencies that are tailored to the specifics the employer wishes to see), a plot (a series of challenges and situations from which you learned things about yourself and demonstrated your ability to achieve), and a strong narrative drive towards a happy ending (your finding a job with organization X). You do not make the employer create a narrative from your application, you provide it for them.

In order to do this you will need to jot down a long list of all your achievements and experiences, and the competencies that you developed while you were doing them (something like a cross between a complete CV and a record of achievement). You then *select* for inclusion only those experiences that fit with the competencies and branding which the employer has told you are required. Remember that beyond the legal requirements to tell employers about criminal

convictions and medical conditions, you are under no obliga-
tion to tell them everything about yourself, so if some fact
about yourself is not relevant to the narrative or employability, it should be left out.

For example, one of the assessment centre candidates we will
meet in Part 4 put it like this:

> It depends on the job. If it is management then I am very much
> into martial arts and I'm a go-getter and I put things like that
> on there. If it is [a more caring profession] I take that off, so yes
> that changes as well. *(Gail)*

Select *and* integrate

In order to make the narrative work, every one of the items
you do select to include should also be made to work as hard
as it can. Employers will be looking for evidence of quite a
number of competencies, but the application form will only
have space for one or two personal statements in which you
provide examples. You should be aware of this and make sure
that you include evidence for the competencies they do not
ask about. Because you are not being asked directly, you have
to do it indirectly by making sure all the information you
include does a number of different things at once. When you
are listing your qualifications or technical skills, for instance,
use this to demonstrate your competencies. For example, in
the IT consultancy's case quoted in the facts section, although
they are looking for very specific technical skills (knowledge
of program languages), they also want to see candidates who
understand that it is the application of skills in a business context that really matters. Successful candidates will therefore
use the space where they have to list all their program lan-

guages as an opportunity to show that they possess the competency of business awareness. Rather than just saying that you have program language X, you would say that you used program language X in order to solve business problem Y.

Equally, when you are listing your extra-curricula activities you should select those that will enhance the impression that you fit with the knowledge brand. Employers are looking for more than something that merely shows that you have a life outside study. They want the activities to integrate with the qualities that are part of their knowledge brand.

Most people who come through will be quite interesting and they'll play football or netball or they'll be a member of a club. You do get an application form where they put things like gym, reading and socializing with my friends but they don't tend to get through. Not because you think 'oh you're not getting through', but because they don't have that oomph factor when you meet them. When you look back on their form you think it was quite clear that that person was probably not going to happen. *(Accountancy firm)*

Despite the fact that reading and gym might convey that you are cultured, interested in the world, understand the importance of fitness, and can self-motivate, they also convey the impression of someone who is happiest being on his or her own. All employers are looking for people who can work in teams to achieve common goals, and it is therefore much better to include group activities.

Also, the greater the range of activities you include (sporting, internships, voluntary, hobbies, employment and travel), the more the employer will infer that you are someone who can handle a number of different responsibilities simultaneously. In the personal statement section, if you refer to only one activity as the arena in which you developed your competencies, you are going to come across as someone who can pursue only a single goal (businesses need people who can manage, plan and organize so that a number of different things can be achieved at the same time).

We've had just about all of the mileage out of his cricket club that we're gonna get, and, frankly, it's not enough. *(Public-sector organization)*

Provide *credible* evidence

The examples you choose should also be credible. In the facts section, one employer pointed out that creating a house washing-up rota or a customer database for Pizza Hut was insufficient evidence of taking initiative. You should have understood by now why the washing-up rota was such a joke to the employer; however, the database example is less clear cut. It may be that this candidate had failed to articulate what a difference the database made to the performance of the restaurant. He or she could have put something more like this. Not only had he or she spotted the need for a database (initiative) and created it (program skills), he or she also worked with the manager to use it as a basis for a marketing campaign (influencing others) and thereby increased turnover by X percent (results driven), so pulling the restaurant up from being the worst performing to being in the top three for its area (business awareness).

This is much more credible. Not only does it integrate a number of competencies within a single question, so covering many bases, it also highlights a serious moment in which a course of action made a tangible and observable difference to the success of the situation. Employers want to see that you take the skills you have acquired as seriously as they do.

Strategy three – do not be tempted to fake it

There are usually two main areas on an application form. There is a facts section and a personal statement section. It is worth pointing out that the facts section *is* a facts section. Undoubtedly the pressure to get an aspirational graduate job can be such that many graduates are prepared to use every trick they can to secure one. The concentration here and in Part 4, on presentational skills and narratives of employabil- ity, might therefore suggest that we are advocating a certain fluidity with factual truth. We are not.

A narrative of employability is not a lie, any more than any presentational skill is a lie. You may not wear the clothes you wear to a job interview every day, but the idea of dressing appropriately in a way that highlights those aspects of your physical appearance which you like and hides those aspects you do not is something that virtually everybody understands and accepts. Narratives of employability are similar in that they are simply an arrangement of facts about yourself in the most attractive and appropriate order for the situation in which you find yourself. It has nothing to do with lying.

In order to answer one of the personal statement questions you might, for example, think of an incident at a workplace which could, on reflection, yield evidence of the growth in your leadership skills. You may not have been aware of this at the time. Indeed, you might only have hit upon it for the purposes of writing an application form. However, there is a big difference between reflecting on this incident for its relevance and the making up of the incident and the workplace, or both. Such mendacity is likely to be cruelly exposed in a panel interview if the assessors decide to pursue it. Interviewers are very good at this because they have seen it all before.

Other facts are even easier to check. When it comes to your age, your GCSEs and A-level grades, your degree class, the university you went to, the jobs you have had and the places you have been, these are a matter of verifiable fact and very easily checkable. However tempting it might be, for example, to massage your degree class upwards, you can be pretty certain that at some point someone is going to ask to see your certificate.

All graduate employers should automatically ask for sight of a degree certificate (although this will also happen if you apply for a temporary job in the financial sector). Anyone tempted to fake a certificate should be aware that obtaining sight of the certificate is the absolute minimum level of verification. The next stage is to check it out with the university itself. To do this the company requires the graduate's permission and, realizing the game is up, this is the point at which many fakers withdraw their application.

Strategic checklist

In order to complete a successful application, you need to be able to answer yes to all the following questions:

- Do you know what competencies this employer requires?
- Have you illustrated as many of them as possible?

- Are you using a range of activities to do so – academic, social, sporting, voluntary, internships and employment?
- Do you know what the employer's knowledge brand is?
- Have you included something that shows how you embody it?
- Have you really answered the questions with credible evidence?
- Has the whole thing been written from scratch?

CHAPTER 7

What to put on application forms – the tactics

Graduate recruiters love mistakes. Nothing thrills them more than receiving an application that is filled with errors of inclusion, presentation, grammar, spelling, punctuation or capitalization. They love it because they do not even have to bother to finish reading the application. They can just put it onto the reject pile, happy in the knowledge that they have just saved themselves and their organization lots of valuable minutes.

The tactics section will therefore concentrate on what will get you deselected, regardless of anything you actually say in your application.

Of course, hardly any recruiters really care about your standard of written English. What bothers them is your standard of professionalism. Graduate recruiters are, by definition, looking for future professionals. They want people they can trust to produce work for clients, customers and colleagues that is not riddled with errors. As they do not know you, all they can do is assess your potential professionalism from what they have in front of them. They reason that if you cannot be bothered to look like a professional at this stage, when you should be doing everything in your power to keep them sweet, what chance is there that you will act like a professional once you are in?

Tactic one: do exactly what they say

The front of the application form says send your CV together with a covering letter. If you don't have a covering letter, even if you are fantastic, you get turned down because you didn't follow the instructions. You have to be quite harsh otherwise you would be interviewing everyone. *(High street bank)*

Tactic two: get someone else to proofread your application

The best tactic you can use to avoid deselection in the initial sift is to make your application forms look like they were written by a potential professional. Anyone who wants to look like a professional will understand that professionals are people who double-check their work, and, if they do not have a particular skill, they organize someone to do the task for them. What this means, in practice, is that any information in sentence form should first be written on your word processor, spell- and grammar-checked there, and then printed off and double-checked by someone whose written English is of a good standard. (That someone is unlikely to be you for the reason that all writing accumulates errors that the writer cannot spot.) Having done this you can then either paste the information into the online form, or print or hand-write it onto the paper form.

Tactic three: avoid non-standard punctuation, capitalization and abbreviations :-(

Email is fast and informal, applying for a job is not. Do not miss out capitals or apostrophes, or use any constructions, either on the form itself or in an email, that you would not use on a traditional hand-written form.

Tactic four: do not go over the word count

Waffling is easy to do online. With a paper application form you might ask yourself how you can fit your life story into such a tiny box. With an open-ended online form you do not know when to stop. Nobody in business has the time to read more than a few paragraphs of anything. When they say 250 words, they mean it.

Tactic five: never hit 'send' prematurely

The long-windedness of the process added to the ability to instantaneously deliver the thing makes it very tempting to send an online application without bothering with all that printing off and double-checking. Never do this. It is worth doing not only because of grammar and spelling. It is also worth doing because you might have failed to delete a joke answer you made to relieve the pressure of all that professionalism.

Tactic six: always keep a copy

You will not remember what you said and you will need to know because you will be asked about it at interview.

Tactic seven: avoid poor handwriting on paper forms

Recruiters can make a case that grammar and spelling are indicative of your potential professionalism, but it is impossible for them to do so with handwriting (PCs and word processors having made handwriting skills completely irrelevant to almost every occupation). Unfortunately for candidates, this makes no difference. Recruiters will make judgements about your professionalism based on the quality of your handwriting. If it is illegible, you will be deselected. If it is scruffy, you are very likely to be deselected. And if it is idiosyncratic, it will raise a question mark, which, when combined with other information, could contribute to getting you deselected.

If you are one of the majority of people whose handwriting is illegible, scruffy or idiosyncratic, you have three possible solutions.

You could scan the form and paste the information from your word processor: the solution that most people adopt. Or you could learn calligraphy. The third option is to get someone to fill it out for you. This, of course, is duplicitous, as the recruiter will now be making judgements about your professionalism based on false information. The only thing to do is write the application as neatly as possible.

Tactic eight: avoid crossings out and correction fluid on paper forms

The second problem with paper forms is that you have only a single copy so any mistakes you make in filling it out will be visible to the sifter, either as correction tape or fluid, or as crossings out. Your primary-school teacher was right, by the way, when she or he said that it is best to delete an error with a single ruled line. Correction fluid never works as well as it should, and many forms are off-white (it is cheaper) so the blob shows up even more. Of course, the best policy is to make no mistakes, but since this is near humanly impossible, it is up to the individual to decide whether the trouble of getting another form is more than the risk of sending off a form that contains obvious corrections. As a basic guide, the number of visibly corrected errors should be less than the number of pages the form contains.

Tactic nine: use the cover letter (and envelope) to ensure you do not get deselected by a temp

Deselection by a temp occurs when you do not include enough information on your cover letter (or on your envelope) to make sure that your application gets to the right person. The post-rooms, internal mail systems and departmental post-opening desks of organizations are often staffed by temps. Only addressing the envelope properly is not enough. At some point in your application's journey through the internal post system of a large organization, the envelope will be removed, almost always before it gets to the desk of the person you sent it to. This is why the letter should include all the address details that were on the envelope (a named addressee, a departmental address for the internal post, as well as the geographical address – because big organizations have more than one office). If you do not have a named addressee, you should phone and get one, and you should always check the spelling as even the most common names can be spelled in different ways. The other thing the letter should include is the highlighted name of the position being applied for or the code or reference, if there is one. Even this is not enough. The first line of the letter should read something like this: 'I am writing to apply for the position of . . .' Your letter should scream (in a very business-like way) precisely where it is going at every opportunity.

Including all these things means that there is now very little chance of your application suffering deselection by a temp (i.e. ending up in the wrong pile on the wrong person's desk in the wrong department in the wrong building in the wrong part of the country).

Tactic ten: apply early

Although there will often be a closing date, it is always better to get your application in early. Rolling recruitment through the year means that if you leave it until the last minute you will be competing for fewer places, and in very bad years you might even end up applying for jobs that no longer exist.

Part

4

How to deal with assessment centres

CHAPTER 8

How to deal with assessment centres – the facts

This then is it. Hundreds of thousands of graduates; employers – each with a few dozen jobs on offer and convinced that they are in a war for talent to fill them; expensive marketing campaigns that control the number and type of applicants; an application process that culls all the graduates who have not worked hard enough and done enough research to put together a decent application (or who did not get the right A-levels). And now the crunch. Can they really pick the future managerial talent based on the utility of your summer holiday experience? Can they predict the future? Or, to put it more precisely, can they predict *your* future?

Probably not, but it is not for want of trying. Throughout this book we have argued that most of what you think you know about graduate recruitment is wrong. The assessment centre (or AC) is the dark heart of graduate recruitment. It is, after all, the source of all those myths we mentioned in the 'Introduction'. And, if the hinterland surrounding the heart had anomalous areas in which things were not quite as they seemed, it should come as no surprise that the centre can be a very strange place indeed.

The rhetoric of the recruitment industry is, however, very certain. The AC, they say, is a rational and objective environment in which the best candidate is scientifically matched to the requirements of the job. It provides, they claim, an objective assessment of your ability to perform under pressure, of your knowledge and skills, of your attitudes and potential, of the competencies you claim, and of your ability to fit in and provide future value to your employer. These things are examined in seven different ways. Some employers will use all seven techniques, others just a few.

The seven techniques

1. Psychometric (aptitude) tests have a single correct answer to each question. You may be examined in numerical or verbal reasoning, in problem solving, a technical or scientific skill, and in things such as spatial and abstract reasoning. These tests are used because employers want to double-check that you do actually have the skills associated with your qualifications.

2. Psychometric (personality) tests in which there is no right or wrong answer – these are really questionnaires designed either to reveal aspects of your personality (such as the way you think or your emotional stability), or to examine aspects of your professional competencies (such as your leadership qualities or attitude to working with others).

3. Individual exercises in which there are better and worse ways to perform (brainstorm activities, case study analysis, in-tray activities) – usually job related and designed to examine things such as your ability to prioritize or to get on top of a brief.

4. Group exercises in which the result is less important than the way that you respond to others in the group – these are usually discussions, problem-solving activities, or group

examinations of case studies, and they are designed to test your ability to influence others in an approved manner.

5. Social events included in the schedule (coffee, lunch, dinner, tours of the premises) – because they are unstructured, these events can cause some candidates to relax and reveal weaknesses that they have otherwise been able to keep hidden. Although this is rarely formally assessed, these events also give assessors a chance to decide whether you will fit in socially and to observe whether you might have the presentational skills to spend time in a similar situation with the organization's clients.

6. Interviews (one-to-one and/or with a panel) are usually designed to examine the competencies that you have claimed in your application and which have not been examined by the other methods.

7. The AC itself – just attending an AC is one long examination of your ability to perform under pressure for several hours, if not a couple of days. This ability to perform consistently under pressure is one of the key requirements of modern management.

What is an assessment centre?

An AC is defined by its mix and range of activities, and by its difference from a single interview as a decision-making event. It is not a place so much as an idea. It does not matter whether the AC is located in an organization's training centre, in its offices, in a hotel or in a conference facility. It also does not really matter whether it all happens in a 48-hour period or whether some of the activities are done online or at a separate event. At its heart, the AC is the idea that if you spread the recruitment decision through time, expand the number and type of assessment activities, use marking and scoring systems to convert what candidates do into a set of figures, and then increase the number of decision makers, you will get a more objective match between the job and the best candidate than you would if you had a single activity (an interview), a single decision maker (the interviewer) and a very brief moment of decision (the first few seconds of the interview).

It is this belief in the rational quality of the decision that makes the AC such a ubiquitous and powerful rite of passage for today's generation of graduates. For, although everyone understands that people can under-perform, or that you can be pipped at the post by another candidate who has that little bit extra, the main claim for the AC is that it *justifies* the choice of one graduate over another.

This is really important for graduate recruiters because there is so much at stake. It is not only that it underpins the whole notion of the war for talent (you can only have a war if you can identify who the talent is). It is not that it makes sense of the diversity agenda (the more objective the decision, the less the outcome is based on prejudice). It is not even that it justifies their knowledge branding (we *know* our people are the best). More than all of this, it justifies the whole point of fast-tracking certain young people through extra training and experiences to positions of responsibility. The whole system of graduate recruitment relies on it being able to objectively recognize the managerial talent of the future. However, simply because it is really important for the AC to appear to be an objective method, it does not mean that it is.

The appearance of objectivity

Look again at the seven techniques used at ACs and you will see that only one of them is genuinely objective: the aptitude tests in which there is a single correct answer. Here the candidate's performance is measured against an objective and external set of absolute standards. Put simply, if you score less than X percent on a numerical reasoning test, nobody will ever give you a job in IT. As we said earlier, these tests are included in the AC as a means of checking that the candidates have the hard skills that their qualifications ought to have given them. This type of test is really a sifting or deselection tool rather than a selection tool. Indeed, this is why it is often these tests that are detached from the AC proper and administered either online or at a separate event.

Of the other five or six methods, the personality questionnaires might appear at first to be another objective means of measuring your traits and attitudes (depending of course on how much store you set by personality profiling). However, what we found was that the recruiters did not really use these tests to determine the outcome. Instead, they were being used as a means of building an impression of the situation but not driving it. For example, they were often used to determine the content of interviews and as a way of confirming or legitimizing decisions that had been come to by other means.

If everyone was almost even you would go back to the psychometrics and say that this person is 90–95 and this person is 60–40 . . . (over 40 is enough to get you through). It is difficult because that was the first time we had done it. I was saying 'she's so nice and everyone really liked her', and the partner I was doing it with said 'but that is the whole point of doing this, because we wanted to get away from taking on people we really like and having people that can do the job as well as be really nice'. (Accountancy firm)

The other main use for the psychometric profiling was to give failing candidates a justifiable reason for why they were not selected.

The remaining five techniques are all more or less subjective because they rely on one set of human beings making decisions about another set of human beings. This is not immediately apparent because of the way the AC uses numerical scores to create the impression of objectivity. Candidates are assigned scores on a four- or five-point scale for their performance in a wide range of skills and attributes and across a wide range of activities. For example, your ability to take action might be scored on something like the following scale:

1. No evidence of action. Blocks or inhibits the proactivity of others. Uses rules and tradition as a way of restricting the initiative of others.

2. Identifies or recognizes what needs to be done or changed, but describes only general intentions, superficial plans or limited action. Only responds to the initiatives of others.

3. Describes clear and specific action points, identifying what needs to be done.

4. In addition to the competence level (3) identifies actions to be taken by others, delegates or involves others in taking actions forward. Describes contingency plans to deal with possible setbacks.

Source: Quoted in The Mismanagement of Talent (Phillip Brown and Anthony Hesketh with Sara Williams, Oxford University Press, 2004).

However, merely assigning a number to something may make it look scientific but it does not in itself turn a subjective evaluation into an objective measurement.

First, it is very difficult for human beings to objectively measure how well other human beings are able to perform any complex task. It is hard enough for people to agree a common standard of judgement for rating a comparatively simple mechanical skill such as surfboarding or ice-skating (and even then the results can look suspiciously idiosyncratic). When rating something as complex as a candidate's ability to influence others, any common standards quickly break down and the actual marking process becomes subjective.

Even if the recruiters are given guidelines, they will still have to interpret them. Should they discuss the guidelines with their colleagues and come to a group consensus, this does not make the process any more objective. The assessors, being human, will disagree about what they saw and about what mark should be awarded. One assessor's observation of leadership skills can always be another's evidence of arrogance.

Assessor 1: *I saw a flicker of 3 behaviour.*
Assessor 2: *If there's some 3 behaviour and some 1 behaviour, don't take the average, mark it as a 1.*
Assessor 1: *I thought we took the maximum behaviour we saw?*
Assessor 2: *No, you don't take the maximum mark, if you see more 2 than 3, mark it as a 2. (Public-sector organization)*

The second problem with objectivity in the AC is that who gets the job is not dependent on any absolute external standard. As we have seen above, the way your performance is measured depends on which recruiter is measuring it. However, crucially, it also depends on the performance of the other candidates they have seen *and* how many jobs there are available. The final result is not only subjective, it is also relative. It is not only dependent on the perceived quality of the other candidates, but also on where the benchmark is set to deliver the approximate number of successful candidates. This means that a candidate who is picked out of one group of candidates for one of two vacancies by one team of assessors might not have been picked for the same job out of another group of candidates by another team of assessors for one of three vacancies a month earlier.

> . . . anything over 3 [is employable] but it tends to be 4s and 5s, depending on what they have got in the rest. Ideally it is 4s and 5s, but realistically, and I would say this year it will be 4s and 5s, last year it would be 3s, 4s and 5s. *(IT consultancy)*

The final problem is the way in which, like the psychometric tests, the apparently objective scores are rarely used by themselves to determine which candidates are offered jobs. For, despite the fact that the recruitment consultancies are constantly coming up with new, more organization-specific and more focused methods for measuring your abilities and potential, most organizations still insist that the decision is made in the way it always has been: by the handful of people who are present at the final washing-up session.

> We don't do best practice, [X] had a fit when he found that's the way we're doing it at the moment where we simply add up all the scores along the top and then do it in a beauty parade-type fashion. But we use scores as a starting point and then talk about the individuals so it gives us the place from which to start looking at the individuals. *(Telecoms company)*

At least one organization does take all your scores in all the various activities, adds them all together, and then offers jobs on the basis of who gets the highest totals. They are not supposed to do this because the methodology of recruitment explicitly forbids this, however, even if we put this aside, it still wouldn't be objective because the people assigning the scores are, of course, well aware of their effect on the final outcome.

The main reason that the real decision is left in the hands of the final interviewers is because the recruiters are loath to lose their influence over who gets the job. Work is social; people need to fit in; managers need to believe that, if their bonus depended on it, you could deliver. Despite all the attempts to measure discrete abilities and aspects of yourself, what is really being assessed is your potential to play the part and fit in. In reality, an AC is more like an audition than it is an examination. Being human, they much prefer to trust their own judgement as to your ability to do this than some consultant's apparently objective measurements of who you are.

In confidence, the recruiters can be very open about this:

> You wonder really that if we picked 150 people who fell out of the hat somewhere and put them through a similar process, would we end up with much different at the end of it? *(High street bank)*

> You've either got it and we'll see it or you haven't. I cannot define it. You just feel it, sense it, you know it when you see it. And you know when it is not there as well. *(Chemical manufacturer)*

Isn't it funny because most people you ask in this business will say to you and they fully believe that when they walk in the door they know the good ones, and people from the business will tell you this as well? Why do we go through all this business? I know them as soon as I meet them, the good graduates, and there is a small part of me that, if you are experienced enough, instinct goes a long way and it has got something to do with cultural issues as well. You just have an innate sense. *(High street bank)*

None of this is to say that there are no advantages to the AC over the old interview-based system. With lots of assessors and the inclusion of line and top management in the process, the AC method means that everybody takes responsibility for talent management and development. It stops power being located in individuals making idiosyncratic decisions and also stops overt sexism and racism degrading the company culture. These benefits are undoubtedly real and important, but they do not justify the exaggerated claims that are made for the ACs' objectivity, which has more to do with the external image of the organizations that use them. We have already high-lighted the way an apparently objective recruitment process can enhance the knowledge brand and the standing of senior management within elite organizations. However, in the context of recruitment, there is perhaps one other, very relevant benefit. An apparently objective process means that the thousands of candidates who walk away from ACs each year without a job do so filled with self-doubt rather than anger.

What all this means for you

Once you get to the assessment centre stage you will almost certainly have what it takes in hard skills to do the job, just like most of the other candidates there. Apart from the aptitude tests concerned with your abilities for these hard, technical skills, all the other tests and activities are an attempt to tease apart differences between you and the other candidates that are to do with your soft skills. This is necessarily subjective and contextual. Whether or not you display evidence of the appropriate soft skills is down to what you say and do, what the person doing the assessing perceives, the performance of the other candidates, and how many jobs there are available.

What this means is that although you can affect the outcome, three out of four of the factors are things over which you have no control. Sometimes you will get the job and sometimes you will not. For every positive interpretation of your performance there is another, equally possible, negative one.

If you look at the following diagram you will see how it is possible for employers to categorize the same candidates in different ways depending on the context. The horizontal axis shows different levels of ability in soft skills while the vertical axis shows increasing and decreasing levels of competence in hard skills. You would think that as long as you got into the top left-hand quadrant (great hard skills *and* great soft skills) you would be guaranteed a job. However, what this diagram shows is that the same candidate can be viewed in two different ways, depending on who is doing the assessing and who the other candidates are. Having great hard skills and great soft skills means that you can either be viewed as an ideal employee (a star) or someone who is just too clever for their own good (a razor). Indeed, you can end up with a job if you end up in three out of the four quadrants. This is because the mix of hard and soft skills you have can always be viewed positively or negatively depending on the context in which you find yourself. The only quadrant you do not want to end up in is the bottom right (poor hard skills and poor soft skills) because nobody in this sector ever gets offered a job.

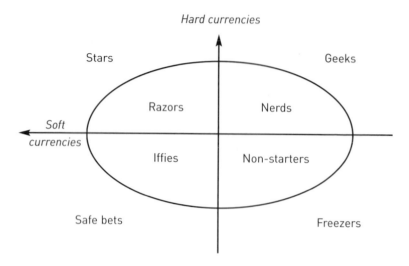

Sometimes you will win, sometimes you will lose – how hard and soft skills combine in the minds of employers

Source: The Mismanagement of Talent (Phillip Brown and Anthony Hesketh with Sara Williams, Oxford University Press, 2004) by permission of Oxford University Press.

Star or razor?

Stars are people who look like they have all the skills the employer requires. They have all the important hard skills, such as A-level results, and the right technical aptitudes, and they also come across as having all the necessary soft attributes. They are good listeners, are confident and articulate but not confrontational, and, because they do not make anyone feel small, they are obviously going to make great leaders. The job offer is automatic.

However, the same candidate can, in a different context, just as easily look like a razor, that is someone who is just too sharp for their own good. The same set of hard skills can be undermined by being seen as someone who fancies themselves a bit too much. Instead of listening to others and working with them on solutions, razors appear to be over-enamoured of their own opinion. No one likes a razor, and they do not get offered jobs.

> . . . in the end we actually question 'Would we want to work for them?' And we decided no, because they were so obsessed about marketing, that marketing was the most important element of any organization. And I was saying, 'What about engineering to support the network?' 'No.' 'IT to build the infra-structure?' 'No.' You just thought he would piss everybody off who he came into contact with. He worked until midnight and he would make everybody else work till midnight and he wouldn't be a right fit for us. *(Telecoms company)*

Safe bet or iffy?

Safe bets are the people who have some but not all of the attributes that employers look for. It is assumed that they are never going to set the world alight, but they are never going to destroy it through their incompetence either. Modern organizations might claim to have very flat management structures, but almost all of them need safe, competent, but not over-ambitious, un-star-like middle managers. It is not exciting to be seen as a safe bet, but they do get offered jobs.

In a different context, the same shortcomings can begin to look very unconvincing. When you have lots of competent candidates the same behaviour will get you labelled an iffy and could lead to rejection. More than any other pair of categories, the difference between the safe bet and the iffy shows how arbitrary the difference between success and failure can be, and it is no wonder that this is the category pair that the recruiters spend most time discussing at the post-AC 'washing-up' session when the jobs get handed out.

> . . . normally a wrap session will take 20 candidates, when you have got rid of the 1s or 2s you might be left with about 60 percent of them, then the 4s and 5s are off and then you are really debating . . . the ones that sit in the middle and we have had maybe two hours tops on about seven or eight people.
> (IT consultancy)

Geek or nerd?

Geeks have lots of hard currencies in terms of the technical skills, such as IT, engineering and high finance, that some organizations really need. And, despite their relative lack of soft currencies, they are seen as having enough social ability and business awareness to work in modern team-centred, sales-aware organizations.

But if the recruiters do not think you can work in a team, then you move category from geek to nerd. In graduate recruitment there are a few roles for geeks, and none for nerds. This is because, just like razors, nerds appear very strong on hard skills and very weak on soft skills.

> You might have somebody, who might be, if they are technically very, very good, and their business skills might [not] be so great. So they might have say scored 4s and 5s and they might have got a 2 in business awareness . . . [and] . . . they have done a very, very technical degree, they haven't had that much business awareness, and we need a few very, very technical people who don't want to work with clients. *(IT consultancy)*

Freezer or non-starter?

These are the people who do not get jobs. So it might seem a matter of indifference as to whether you are rejected as a freezer or as a non-starter. It could however be important. Freezers are people who are seen to have failed to perform on the day. This is usually put down to stage fright. Non-starters are seen as people who have somehow got through to the AC under false pretences and who have no real right to be there. They would never stand a chance, however many times they tried. While being seen as a freezer is just a more charitable explanation for the same behaviour, it is obviously much better to walk away thinking that you could have been a contender than it is to walk away having been characterized as someone who would never have made it anyway.

Conclusion

What all of the above should have demonstrated is that ACs are not objective, they are not scientific and, at certain points, the results can be arbitrary. Clearly, no employer needs to measure the difference between a star and a geek. The recruiters know perfectly well who is who (and they do not need 48 hours of an AC to spot it). The problem comes when they are trying to decide between whether you are a star or a razor, or, more likely, between whether you are a safe bet or an iffy. What happens then is that tiny differences between the way candidates present themselves, and small subjective differences between what the assessors are looking for, bounce back and forth through a hall of mirrors to the point where they become magnified out of all reality and proportion. It is then that an either/or decision is made. They decide whether you are one or the other, employable or not employable, a star or a razor, a safe bet or an iffy, a geek or a nerd, and, if you clam up, whether you will walk away feeling like a freezer or a nonstarter. Which side you fall into is likely to affect your life for a very long time. In the next chapter we will show you what you can do to respond.

CHAPTER **9**

How to deal with assessment centres – the strategies

The following is one strategy you could choose:

It is great that you don't have to tell people the truth because you lie so much at interviews.

At the most recent one I found out all about the project that they were running, found out the philosophies that they had, found out through people that had already worked there, were they male or female, what panel would be interviewing me, and really geared it to that. Went in there saying that I couldn't work for a company that didn't have the philosophy that they had, that I agreed with their policy . . . so really just covered all my thoughts and beliefs on the sheets that they provided and I asked them to provide me with the literature and they did so, and I just looked at it and went in there to be that person that they wanted. But I didn't believe any of it.

When I go for interviews, if they ask about family I seldom mention my mum at all and in fact I just tell them that I have been brought up by my father and I don't even mention that my mum ever exists, because if they then quiz me about my father I know everything that he has done is acceptable. He owns the £200,000 house, he drives flash cars and he is in the right job

▶

but my mother lives in a council house and is a care assistant and I know that wouldn't go down too well. So I just omit the fact that she exists.

That is what it is like with interviews and jobs, you have to say the right things. I don't think that some of the interviews and some of the jobs, they are not going to the true person, they are getting what they want to hear and because we know what they want to hear, we are telling them that. *(Gail)*

This is another:

The bank was one of the best assessment centres I've been to so far because at the end of it the Chief Executive of the whole bank came down. He said that they view this process as more important than a lot of things that they do in the business and that he hoped that we won't go away bitter or gutted that we didn't get the job, because, ultimately, if you didn't get the place you're not the person that we're looking for. And you'd rather know that before you go into the job. The worst thing is going into a job that you hate. And he was very right in what he was saying.

The fact that they are taking one in four people makes you think to yourself that you've got as good a chance as anybody else. I don't know if I was competing against people. I was just trying to put across who I was, and again if that isn't what people were looking for then fine, I'm not the person for the job and I accept that, it's not something that I relish and think to myself, well why didn't they take me in and blame them for everything, it's sort of now I realize that if I'm not good enough, then I'm not good enough, or if I'm not the type of person they are looking for, then I'm not the type of person they are looking for. *(Douglas)*

Gail and Douglas are not typical graduates. Gail is 31. She was a latecomer to higher education with a wide range of business and public-service experience on her CV; she had also studied psychology at university and this, despite her never having been to a full AC, gave her an insight into recruitment methodologies. Douglas is at the other extreme. A deeply committed Christian, at 21 he was a veteran of two ACs in the finance sector. He had considerable faith in the ability of the AC to match the job to the candidate.

Gail and Douglas are real people. They were competing against each other at an AC for entry to a management training scheme in a public-sector organization.

The two of them might not be typical but they are archetypal. They represent the twin extremes of the two strategies that are currently being used by graduates who want to secure themselves aspirational jobs. We call the two strategies 'Player' and 'Purist'. These are the two strategies in a nutshell: if you are a Player, you do everything you can to turn yourself into the person they want to hire; if you are a Purist, you do everything you can to stay true to yourself.

It is at the AC where things begin to diverge. Up to this point, all the strategies or tactics we have suggested can be adopted by more or less everyone. Perhaps you might have felt that developing narratives of employability bordered on the disingenuous, or you might have felt that basing a recruitment strategy on any form of self-fulfilment rather than on employer requirements was spectacularly naive. But these differences are ones of emphasis rather than anything more profound. At the AC, however, all this has changed, and two very different strategies are being employed and you are going to need to choose between them.

To illustrate the difference we are going to follow two Players (Gail and Gus) and three Purists (Douglas, Maureen and Terry) as well as other graduates through the AC process, showing what they do differently.

The Players

This is Gus. At 22, Gus is less cynical than Gail but, despite his relatively poor A-level results and his engineering degree from one of the less prestigious universities, he has the insight into his car manufacturer AC that makes him a true Player.

I think that it comes down to this: the impression you make when you walk into a room and the first thing that comes out of your mouth. I think it is very important and I think you could probably study it for a hundred years. I know myself, having done interviews for people, not to that sort of level but doing interviews, they were hired or not hired. They generally had the job within four seconds and they could then only lose it.

The fact is, with the interview, if you have got someone sitting there [at the wash-up session] going no, no, he's really good, he's really good at this, he's really good at that. Even if you had an average mark in all of those tests I think you are alright and I think that is why I was in that last eight, because the first interview went like that and I think that the lady who did it was pretty impressed with me.

I think it is all relative and I think all those tests are used to back up personal opinions. I don't know exactly how they work but I guarantee that [the three people offered jobs] are not [the people who got] the top three marks on all of those tests. I feel pretty confident about that. (Gus)

This is the secret war at the heart of graduate recruitment. On the one side are the Players. Sussed and worldly wise. If you are one of the Players, you try to extract all the leverage you can from your situation, modifying your appearance, accent, background, and taking what advantage you can of your gender in order to get the job you want. You can do this because either intuitively or through experience you have come to understand what we discovered through observation: that graduates are not being selected for aspirational jobs on the basis of the latest objective recruitment methods, but by the oldest of instinctive reactions. The Players have understood that all that talk of finding the right fit between the candidate and the role is just so much talk, even when it comes from the mouth of the Chief Executive of a high street bank. Players know that there are more matching candidates than there are prestigious roles, and you are going to do everything in your power to get the job.

One of the most impressive things about the Player strategy is the way that it has propagated itself entirely by word of mouth. There are no company brochures, careers-service leaflets or recruitment publications telling you to dissemble. Instead, there is a vast underground pool of Player advice which, like the rumours about what really goes on at ACs, percolates itself through the graduate community, finding its way into the minds of people who are looking for the edge that will help them get the job they want.

This is another of Gail and Douglas's competitors for the public-sector training scheme: 'Would anyone who knows me have recognized me in the interview?' he asked himself. 'They would have thought some of the things I said were a bit, kind of, bit over the top, like my playing up my degree of commitment to the job and saying that if I didn't get in I'd definitely spend the next year trying to work my way up the grades and things like that, which I wouldn't necessarily have done . . . well I might have. But all my really good friends have been telling me for ages that I've got to go along to interviews and basically *not* be myself. They are all more successful in interviews and things than I am and they all say you've got to go along and tell them what they want to hear.'

The Purists

This is Maureen. She is 24, privately educated, and has 10 As at GCSE, four As at A-level, a first degree from a top-ranked university and a PhD in English literature. Her first AC was for one of the most prestigious government departments. She shares Douglas's faith in the fairness of the recruitment process.

There is an element of personal PR, you can go there, not exactly show off, but really do your best and show what you can do and really try to impress, but be yourself. So if you do get the job then you know that it's your sort of job, you're not just randomly picked. It's not a lottery. You're not just picked by the fact that you've got good grades, but because you genuinely will be the right person for the job.

It's going to be real pressure, it's going to be fairly scary I think, but not in a way because the assessment seems quite fair, it does seem to take into account a lot of things to give you a really good chance of showing yourself in the best possible light, rather than trying to catch you out, and I think it should be quite an interesting challenge. There will be sort of team work within the group rather than competing against each other. Hopefully people will actually realize that they're probably not competing against each other, because everyone's going for different things anyway and you might as well work together.

It's best to be yourself in the sense that you will survive best because you won't have to keep trying to remember, you know, what you're trying to put across, and also because if you get through and hate the job, then it's your own fault and you are also depriving someone else who could do it better, so although it would be hard to take in the very short term, in the long term, if I don't get it, I've been myself and done my best and therefore it wasn't the job for me and I'd be pleased that I would be able to say that rather than always thinking maybe if I [had not] been myself it would have been better, you know. *(Maureen)*

Purists like Maureen are on the other side in the secret war. If you are a Purist, you believe that what is important about work is not the salary, nor the esteem the work brings, but how personally fulfilling you find it and whether it suits your unique mix of experiences and attributes. You therefore accept the new, apparently objective, recruitment methodology at face value because it gives you an opportunity to find out whether you will be suited to a particular role and a particular organization. You use the selection process as a way of finding out about yourself. While not welcoming failure, you are reconciled to it because it gives you the opportunity to find out what sort of person you really are. This is the *reductio ad absurdum* of the Purist strategy: you try to feel grateful for being rejected.

The war between Player and Purist is undeclared. Partly this is because much of what the Players get up to is kept quiet from all but their best, most like-minded friends, and partly it is because some Purists simply do not believe that playing is possible.

This is Terry, another Purist, whom we will meet again in Part 5.

> You know you have to just be who you are really. And if they are not looking for someone like you then, well, that is the best way to go into it I think. Just be yourself. There is no point in trying to model yourself on someone else you have met or whatever.
>
> I think that some people go in there with a kind of over-inflated version of themselves. But I don't think I have ever, ever met anybody who I thought was playing or play acting, making themselves something that they are not. I think that if you do, if someone like me can see it then the assessor can see it. *(Terry)*

But Terry, of course, cannot see it. Douglas, however, is a declared Purist who suspects that something else is going on, perhaps because he recognizes a little bit of Player in himself.

> Assessment centres get more out of people than one interview. You can blag an interview, I think that's the best way of putting it, if you want to. You can come across all rosy, but in an assessment you come across as your real self, you're not given the time to do anything else, you know, you do come across as your real self.
>
> However, you've an idea what they're looking for and you try to match that, whether or not you are that type of person. I mean I tried to be as honest as I possibly could be, but I'm sure there were people there who were trying to be something that they're not to try and get the job. Now I don't know if that comes across, or if that's recognized, but you know you can tell who's an out-

going person generally in public, but whenever you go to an event like that everyone tries to up their levels to be something that maybe they're not. I don't know, because I don't know an awful lot of people outside the event, but it's just the impression that I got. *(Terry)*

Why the Player strategy works

Being a Player works because assessors want to see examples of soft attributes and skills that are almost entirely unverifiable in any objective sense and which can only be assessed in the mind of the beholder. They can, therefore, be faked if the candidates have the right social knowledge or personal adaptability to do so. Choosing to be a Player allows you to appear suitable for more jobs than the Purists and thus gives you more throws of the dice, even if your chances of getting any particular job may diminish slightly (because playing is harder to do). Your short-term problem is that recruiters generally believe their own rhetoric and want to employ Purists. The disadvantage of playing is when you get found out.

Why the Purist strategy works

Despite the option to fake it, being yourself is always going to be easier than playing. So, although choosing to be a Purist will make you suitable for fewer jobs, you may have a slight advantage over everyone but the very best of Players if you find yourself at an AC that does suit who you are. Your big short-term disadvantage is that if you get rejected it has to hurt because you always put your true self on the line.

These are, of course, ideal strategies. There are very few people who are all Player or all Purist. You will probably move between the two according to circumstances. You might be more of a Player when you are being interviewed and more of a Purist when you are completing a personality questionnaire. Or you might be more of a Player at an AC for an organization that you do not really believe is for you, and more of a Purist when you are in line for the job you really want. Or the other way around. What is essential is that you recognize which strategy you are using and why.

So how do you choose which one to use? In a moment, we shall ask you a series of questions that might help you towards making a decision. But following, in a nutshell, are the two strategies, their advantages and disadvantages.

Purists in a nutshell

The only strategy I have is to be me, and if they don't want me then I don't want to work for them. *(Samuel)*

If you are a Purist, you believe that there is a best person for the job and that the AC is there to find the best match between the available candidates and the role. You are very likely to have been convinced by the recruitment industry rhetoric into believing in the objectivity of the texts and exercises, and may even see your job as a candidate as being to help the recruiters in finding that person (even when it is not you!). Even if you are not fully convinced that the tests are objective, you will still tend to believe that the recruiters know what they are doing. So, while you will try to perform to your best, you do not attempt to hide aspects of yourself or try to be someone you are not in order to get the job. You understand that it is difficult to be yourself in an AC because you are nervous and under pressure. However, you still try to give a true sense of who you really are, and all you are prepared to do is make some relatively minor adjustments to the way you present yourself. Indeed, you view anything else as at best cheating and at worst industrial sabotage.

We will look at creating a narrative in more detail in the tactics section, but, if you are a Purist, you are someone who believes deeply in your own narrative of employability. Or, to put it another way, you believe in your own narrative to the extent where you do not really believe it can be altered.

This could be for two reasons. You might be someone who has always wanted to work as a Y in organization X, sometimes from a very young age, and so have directed your energies towards that end. Or you might be someone who, while you are less specific in your long-term ambition, nevertheless has a strong belief in your own capabilities and destiny, so much so that you do not perceive your narrative of employability to be anything other than a statement of your authentic self.

If you are a Purist, you tend to believe strongly in the idea that life is a meritocracy. This belief has brought you success at school and university, and you view an AC as just another technical, exam-like challenge in which those who succeed deserve their rewards. To this end, you will tend to accept that a negative result at an AC means that you were not right for the job or right for organization X.

ADVANTAGES OF BEING A PURIST

- It is the most stress-free strategy, as you avoid the difficulties of pretending to be someone you are not and so can never be found out.

- If you are offered a job, it will provide an enormous boost to your self-esteem and to your sense of having a privileged destiny.

- Rejection can be seen as an opportunity to gain some valuable information about who you really are and what sort of job would really suit you.

RISKS OF BEING A PURIST

- Not getting the job might lead to you questioning whether you are capable of something you really want to do.

- You narrow the range of possible jobs you can reasonably go for.

- You might find the behaviour of the Players difficult to come to terms with and so find group activities demoralizing.

- You might find it hard to construct a convincing narrative of employability as you do not believe it is right to leave some things about yourself out of it.

- Over-investing in the feedback can be a problem for Purists, so do not be demoralized if some organizations do not treat it as seriously as you do.

- The biggest risk is that a Player will get the job ahead of you.

- Because you are relying on being natural, you might not appreciate that you need to spend as much time as possible polishing your own narrative of employability

- Just because you are a Purist does not absolve you of the responsibility for making the connections for employers between your experience and the skills they are after.

The Player strategy

Players are called Players because, instead of seeing the AC as a meritocratic, objective process, they see it as a game in which the only object is to win. If you are a Player, you will therefore obscure or highlight any and every aspect of yourself which you can bring under your control in order to secure the job: your clothes, your hobbies, your answers to personality questionnaires, how much you smile and so on. Some Players are even prepared to lie, but this is not really what playing is about (and if you are tempted to lie you should review the consequences as laid out in Part 3). As a Player, you take what experience and qualifications you have and create and act out different narratives of employability according to the needs of all the different organizations you apply to. At the AC, your sole aim is to convince the recruiters that you are the candidate who best fits the role.

ADVANTAGES OF BEING A PLAYER

- Because you can apply for any job, you maximize your chances of getting one.
- Your narratives of employability will be well prepared and well rehearsed.
- If you are good at it, you will have an advantage over even the most suitable Purist because you are more adaptable.
- Rejection is not hurtful to your sense of self, indeed it is a learning process that improves your performance in the next AC.

RISKS OF BEING A PLAYER

- Being bad at playing is about the worst thing you can do at an AC.
- You might end up in a job you hate.
- It might be difficult to be yourself if you do get into the organization.
- You face ethical dilemmas regarding how far you are prepared to go and may be tempted to tell a direct lie.

Players and Purists: an apologia

What we are not saying, however, is that Players are dastardly winners and Purists are naive losers. Most of the Players are not telling direct lies (although there is a lot of evidence to show that many people do elaborate, exaggerate and lie on application forms). All you are doing by playing is trying to live up to the salary and success expectations that you have for yourself and that other interested parties (such as your creditors and your parents) demand of you. In your determination to avoid the consequences of the graduate glut, you feel you have no choice but to try all that you can to secure the job. The secret advantage that you have found is to slip between the rhetoric of the recruitment industry and its reality. The recruiters want evidence of specific soft skills, so you provide it. The fact is that it is the recruitment industry's pursuit of the pseudo-science of soft-skill measurement that has allowed you to do this.

Equally, Purists are not saints. In some ways, if you are a Purist, you are exploiting the recruitment industry's investment in psychometric tests and character-revealing assessments for your own ends, in order to find out who you really are. Purists, we found, are just as likely as Players to apply to as many employers as possible during the application stage. They just see it differently: the Players see it as a way to assess their position in the market, the Purists see it as a means of finding out about their strengths. Nor can we find any difference in ambition, abilities or commitment. Purists want success just as badly as Players. And neither are Purists naive. The whole Purist approach is not fundamentally misguided. Of course it is better to be offered a job on the basis of an assessment of your real self. Of course it is better to be in a job that you are suited to and which you enjoy. The brilliance of the Purist strategy is its simplicity: find a job that matches your talents, be who you are. And because it requires no dubious duplicity, the strategy is available both to those with strong ethical standards and to those made uncomfortable by having to perform. The only fly playing around in the Purist ointment is the fact that for every remunerative, fulfilling graduate job there are perhaps 20 or more graduates interested in filling it.

Caveats on Players and Purists

Nor does any of this mean that being a Purist is a poor strategy or that the Purists are losing the competition for jobs to the Players. The playing strategy only allows candidates to go for jobs that they would not naturally be considered for if they applied as their real selves. Playing is just a way of shortening the odds on getting an aspirational job. It is not a way to guarantee that you win. It is also, of course, much more risky than being a Purist. As a Purist, you might fail to give a good account of yourself, but you can never be caught out failing to *be* yourself. As a Player, you are always in danger of being found out, and while a good Player can beat a strong Purist candidate some of the time, a poor Player, if and when you are caught, will always lose.

Questions to ask yourself when deciding whether to be a Player or a Purist

There are two broad questions you should ask yourself when considering whether you are going to approach an individual AC as a Player or a Purist. Do you think it is right to play and, if so, can you pull if off? Again, this is not to suggest that being a Player is the better strategy, this is just the best way round for the questions to be asked.

DO YOU THINK IT IS RIGHT TO PLAY?

- Outside the usual codes of formality, is it acceptable to present a false picture of yourself in order to get an aspirational job?
- Do you think you know better than the assessors whether you will be the best person for the job?
- Do you think an AC is a competition?
- Is it worth hiding an aspect of yourself if you think it will help you succeed?
- If you were rejected, would it make sense to apply again?

CAN YOU PULL IT OFF?

- Are you a natural performer?
- Do you have an instinctive grasp of the best way you should present yourself in other situations (because this one will be far more challenging)?
- Constructing a self for the benefit of someone else is hard work and can be very stressful. Do you cope well enough under pressure to do it?
- Being bad at playing is about the worst thing you can do at an AC. Are you prepared to accept the risk that you will fall flat on your face and blow your chances?
- Have you thought ahead (even if you do succeed there is always the danger that you might end up in a job you hate while it might also be difficult to be yourself once you're there)?

You should consider playing only if the answer to both these broad questions is yes. Otherwise, being a Purist will always be your best strategy.

Know your competitors

Remember that whatever strategy you choose, you still need to know what the other side is doing. If you are a Purist, you need to be aware of exactly what you are up against. You need to understand how well rehearsed the Players are. You need to know that there are people out there who will change their accent, use their sexuality and adjust every aspect of their experience in order to get the jobs that actually would be perfect for you. This should make you realize that, if you are going to make a success of the Purist strategy, you have to try as hard as they can to give the best account of yourself. If you are a Player you need to understand what Purists are like because you have to convince the assessors that you too are a Purist. Outside the most aggressive sales roles, very few graduate recruiters want to employ Players. Whatever you have chosen, you will benefit from studying the other's strategy.

10

How to deal with assessment centres – the tactics

In Part 3, we showed that one of the most powerful ways you can convince recruiters of your suitability is to think in terms of a narrative of employability. As you will remember, a narrative of employability is no different from any narrative. It has a hero (you) with estimable qualities (a combination of hard, technical skills and soft, character-based qualities that are tailored to the specifics the employer wishes to see), a plot (a series of challenges and situations from which you learned things about yourself and demonstrated your ability to achieve), and a strong narrative drive towards a happy ending (your finding a job with organization X).

In the first, application stage of the recruitment process, we suggested you could construct a narrative of employment by selecting or suppressing those facts that were relevant to the employer you were applying to. However, it is one thing to construct a narrative of employability on a CV or application form, it is quite another to live up to it in person, and this, perhaps more than anything, is the entire point of the AC. It is the place where your ability to *perform* the narrative will be tested.

The narrative of employability approach works so well at the AC because employers respond to these narratives in a deeply human way. This is partly because your narrative flatters their own narratives of employability, and partly it is because it gives them a way of unconsciously assessing all those difficult-to-measure soft presentational skills that have become so important in recruitment. In the tactics section we will therefore look at the AC from the point of view of performing your narrative of employability. The tactics below include different approaches for both Players and Purists and remain true whether you are merely putting the finishing touches to your own authentic narrative or creating one almost entirely from scratch. We will divide this section into four different aspects (the hero, the hero's estimable qualities, the plot and the happy ending) and show how employers respond to and how they assess each part of your narrative. It is important to remember, however, that the narrative works as a whole and that its success is as much to do with your confidence in performing the narrative as it is with any single aspect.

Apart from the tactics listed below, you will also find that the narrative of employability is a useful way of thinking about and organizing all the other pieces of advice you will have received on ACs.

The hero

The way you appear to others sets the standard for their expectations of you. In order to be picked by organization X you will either need to be like its graduate employees already, or be prepared to adjust your image towards them. They are organization X's graduate brand and, like them, you must embody that brand in order to succeed. Remember, one of the key things you are being judged on at an AC is the ability to convey the knowledge brand in person, and the more elite the job, the more this is going to be true. The recruiters must absolutely trust you to walk into a room with their key clients and look and act like a member of the team that the client has bought. You must, therefore, realize that throughout the AC almost every aspect of your appearance, your demeanour and your behaviour is being examined. They may not be being scored directly, but they are being watched consciously and unconsciously all of the time you are there.

It's not something we are going to measure, but we are human . . . if someone comes in and they are confident and articulate and they are dressed smartly you are going to have a favourable impression of them immediately. To come out with crap, you are going to look for evidence to say 'Well there is nothing there of substance'. But you have got a favourable opinion immediately. You know we are human. *(Telecoms company)*

Preparing for being the hero

Players and Purists prepare differently. The following is a typical Purist reaction to the idea of preparing for an AC: 'You can't really practise to present yourself in a certain way, if you are a certain person that is the way you are. But I think the only thing you can build on is your confidence, maybe that is what really puts people through. I believe with the tests a bit of practice would really help. But as regards interviews, I think being confident helps more.'

The danger here for Purists is under-preparation. If you have invested in being yourself, it is easy to worry that too much preparation might lead you towards trying too hard and tempt you into remembering specific things to say or tactics to pursue. Remember that being a Player or a Purist is really a strategy for coping with soft-skills assessment. There is nothing wrong, as a Purist, with practising your hard skills by preparing for the aptitude tests or by mugging up on factual details about the company in preparation for interview. Indeed, you must always do this.

Players, however, have two choices. As a Player, you can either prepare as completely as possible or avoid the costs of preparation and attempt to create your persona on the day (a strategy that is known by the world at large as blagging). This was Gus's strategy at the car manufacturer AC. His work experience as an electronics goods salesman and the fact that he had once been offered a trading role with a major investment bank in the City (which fell through) suggest that he has enough confidence to adapt himself on the day.

I'm not really into these seminars about interview techniques. I have only ever once not got a job that I have gone to the interview for so I must be pretty reasonable. I don't do any preparation apart from look on the Internet. Generally if you take a car manufacturer, I know what they do; it's in my head anyway. A few specific names might go out of my head but I read the papers and I sort of keep up with what is going on. *(Gus)*

As we saw at the start of this section, Gail is a different type of Player. She prepares by trying to match herself both to the assessors and to the role. For her public-sector AC she went to the trouble of actually meeting a manager in the same organization beforehand.

I know someone who used to be a Director and who is a friend, and I rang him up when I got this interview and he said 'I'll put you in touch with a friend who is already a manager' [in the same organization]. So he put me in touch and I went along there and she gave me some guidance notes for people who wanted to go to the top. It was all very business orientated and so I power dressed with a briefcase and went in there very business orientated, in the same manner which this other business manager had presented herself to me. *[Gail]*

Undoubtedly, the more preparation you do, the better your chances. Only the most confident Players should risk following Gus's blagging tactic (and it would be wise to adopt it only when you have a number of other ACs lined up already).

Appearance

Gail's use of the power suit and the briefcase shows how seriously she takes the idea of matching her appearance to the knowledge brand identity of the individual employer. It is the specificity here that is important. As a Player, Gail is not merely trying to look professional. She will not power dress and carry a briefcase to every AC. She will do so only at those ACs where she identifies the graduate brand as particularly corporate in style.

In contrast, the Purist approach to appearance is one of generic professionalism. This is Maureen again:

I had to buy a suit because I've never had a suit, so I bought a little suit from Next. I'm just going to look smart as if I was giving a paper for a conference, but not completely unnaturally so smart that I just never would wear [it] in real life as it were, because to some extent I want them to judge me as I am really. But I'd like them to see me and obviously I will, you try and put a certain . . . You do try to give them what they want to some degree. Equally I don't want to get a job just because I've managed to act out a role for a day; it's not in the long term. I'd like to think that as long as someone is dressed appropriately and looks reasonably smart then that would be enough, they wouldn't judge on anything else. They're only human, I'm sure they have some preference to one or the other, but hopefully it wouldn't affect them too much. *(Maureen)*

This is the one area, however, in which some of the female Purists do show more Player-like behaviour. This is perhaps because they have more decisions to make than the men, and many women we interviewed had agonized about how to wear their hair, the amount of make-up they should use, and whether to wear trousers or a skirt. But again, their approach is not thought through tactically in the sense of being related to the specifics of the employer's knowledge brand. Their decisions seem to be based more on an instinctive approach to how they should look.

In fact, if you are a Purist who is tempted to flirt with a little playing, thinking through your appearance and adjusting it towards the brand in this way is one of the easiest ways you can do it. No one will ever know, and it will have a positive subliminal effect on your assessors. Indeed, if you do get the job, it is almost certain you will end up dressing like this anyway.

Accent

Accent more than anything else is the one aspect of themselves that a lot of Players admit to changing. 'I'm often attempting to match the person I am talking to,' said one. 'I may put on a slightly more public-school voice, I don't know'. Another put it like this: 'I tend to go to my Harrogate accent when I'm in interview, because I did this thing about it in English language, because if you do have this lilt in the accent, like you do, and if you, say, soften your accent to make it sound more like theirs then it's called a "convergence of accents" and that is supposed to be a sign – kind of breaking down barriers between people.'

Gus told us that he could change his accent:

> . . . so that it actually sounds a bit more, a bit posher let's say, but I can also do it the other way as well. It depends on the company that you are in. I think generally in an interview situation I just go for the middle unless there is something that is really, really obvious and it has got to be proper and then I'll be conscious of being very proper. So, for example, when I had that merchant bank interview that was a situation where it needs to be very proper because the people you are speaking to are, they are your ex-public schoolboys. It is very important to them that they work with people that are that way, so I suppose you sort of become that way. *(Gus)*

Naturally, Douglas and the other Purists would have none of this conscious style shifting.

> I know I've got a strong accent, but again, as I say, I'm not both-
> ered. If people are fussed by what accent I've got, not neces-
> sarily about what I'm articulating, but more accent, then I'm
> not bothered, you know. It's one of those things, if the job's for
> you, the job's for you, if it's not, it's not. *(Douglas)*

Accent more than anything highlights the problems over the whole diversity agenda we discussed in Part 1. Although Gus talks about being able to rough up his accent, most of the Players are emphasizing the ability to take their accent up-market. (The candidate quoted about putting on what she calls her Harrogate accent is also talking about shifting up: Harrogate is posh Yorkshire.) In order to do this successfully, you need to avoid obviousness and caricature, and to achieve this you have to have received quite a lot of exposure to the ways of the middle and upper-middle classes. This is not available to everyone, and this reinforces the idea that the opportunity to play successfully, and so shorten the odds of success, is not available to all. A strong regional accent restricts your options. If you are a Player with a strong regional accent that you cannot modify, you have no choice but to be a Purist in this regard. One tactic you might be able to use would be to draw attention to the organization's espoused diversity agenda and subtly hint that you were attracted to the organization because of it.

Gender

Many female Players are well aware of how playing up gender markers can alter their chances. However, they are often embarrassed by this because it goes against the meritocratic ideology they have been brought up on. 'This sounds really awful,' said one, 'but I think being attractive, looking good and looking pretty and having a nice smile on the face does help. It depends, it sounds terrible, but it depends on the sex of the employer and the sex of the interviewer sometimes . . . I mean basically I would imagine . . . and I think . . . What the hell! I think it does matter, yes.'

'However bad this sounds,' said another female candidate, 'there's a huge advantage because a lot of the interviewers are male and if you're a female without doubt it puts you at a slight advantage. Well, male interviewers feel a lot more inclined towards the female candidates and are a lot more friendly and easy-going, and they almost still have the stereotype that girls won't be as capable as the guys because they're a lot nicer and then they realize as you're doing answers that you're quite a good candidate.'

Gail, of course, is well aware of this, but even she has her limits (although they may be less to do with ethics than with an awareness of appropriate dress in a professional environment).

If you are in a panel [interview] and [one of them] is a male and you pay too much attention, and in both my interviews I have monitored this, if you have got two females and a good-looking male, then you don't want to pay attention to the male . . . because I feel there will be a [reaction]. I mean you have always to refer to someone of the same sex and that is what I go on, and studies have proved that, if you are being interviewed by a male and female, when you answer the question you reply to the same sex interviewer and that is what I tend to do as well.

I remember studying a research project a while ago and it was on attractiveness and one of the themes was about whether

▶

they use sexuality to get jobs and they do, but . . . that would be a dangerous ground for me so I would go as far as, I would change my dress to power dress to any stage but if I was looking feminine and tight tops and things, I am not sure I would go that way . . . if it was to wear low tops and things I wouldn't go that way. *(Gail)*

From the male side, it is wise to be aware that many recruiters are women and that excessive displays of machismo or arrogance are perceived as evidence that you lack sensitivity to the importance of interpersonal abilities.

The hero's estimable qualities

Your estimable qualities will be examined in the various scored tests and activities held at the AC. The first area that will be examined is likely to be your aptitude for the hard, technical skills relevant to your employer. As we said above, these must always be practised whether you are a Player or a Purist.

TO PREPARE FOR APTITUDE TESTS AND INDIVIDUAL EXERCISES, YOU WILL NEED TO . . .

- find out what sort of tests will be given – you should be told but you can always ask;
- buy a relevant test practice book (there are many available);
- practise the tests under timed conditions – get someone to help you do this and help mark them (it makes it more real);

- read the instructions on the day and quickly scan the whole test to see what and how much you have to do;

- divide the number of questions by the time you have to do them (although you should be aware that some of these tests are deliberately designed so that they cannot be finished in the time available);

- keep checking that the line you are filling in on the answer sheet matches the question you are answering (easy to get wrong and devastating if you do).

The second set of qualities that will be examined is your soft skills. Evidence for these will be looked for in the psychometric tests and in the various role-plays, group activities and individual exercises.

Tactics for psychometric tests (personality)

As we said in the facts section, we do not believe that the personality tests are really being used to make decisions about you. This means that how you approach personality tests comes down to your personal strategy. Some candidates are scrupulously honest (Purists of course), others tweak their answers towards what they think the employer wants to see, while some attempt to fake as much as they can (guess which!). The consultants who devise the tests claim to have sophisticated ways of spotting dishonesty. This may be true.

Tactics for group exercises and activities

The group exercise is one of the most important assessments at the AC. It is completely unreal; it is inherently stressful because the room is full of people with clipboards recording your every word you know you have to contribute otherwise you will not be scored; and this may also be the one point in the whole AC where all the assessors watch your performance together and so have the same information to go on when they make their decision. It is also almost impossible to prepare for. Purists, however, should know that this is the point in the AC where it will become apparent who the biggest Players are and that, as such, you should be prepared to feel an additional load of irritation at their behaviour.

One guy in our group was particularly forceful in putting his view across and very unwilling to compromise, which became quite difficult, but he did back it up with some really good points, and it was clear that he thought it was important that he was seen not to back down. I think the rest of us felt that it would have been easier if he just veered a little bit, but he felt that that line was one he was going to take. Maybe he wouldn't have done, maybe he would have been more willing to compromise if it had been less competitive, that was the only time I felt really that anyone's personal interests have intruded. Everyone's been really supportive and our group actually has been quite friendly. *(Maureen)*

What employers say about group exercises

I don't think it is rocket science really. You notice in the group exercises it is people who don't rush to take the offensive, it is people who aren't aggressive, it is people who are able to simply engage in just general conversation who will laugh, it is about body language as well. There is a lot of fun and it is a big thing for me, body language at assessment centres. The blokes on the group exercises who do all their arm waving and all this sort of business are very kind of negative. *(High street bank)*

. . . one of the problems we have with people from X university is that they seem to have a lot of coaching and they have the really good careers advisory service that a lot of them use and they are told all the different things they need to be doing in their group exercise. They are told be the timekeeper, make sure everyone speaks, don't talk over people . . . So you think if the person has been clever enough or has been coached to be contrived and to sit in a group exercise and say 'Oh that was a very good point, what do you think?' to the person who hasn't said much, you can't really mark them down for that even though you know they've been coached. But they've learned it. You can't mark someone down for that. *(Car manufacturer)*

ESSENTIAL THINGS TO DO IN GROUP EXERCISES

- You must contribute or you cannot be scored: they can only assess what they can see and hear.
- You must aim your contribution at the others in the group and not at the assessors so it should naturally emerge from the conversation.
- Do not talk over anyone.
- Do not shout at all or gesticulate too much.
- Do not give any impression that you think the activity absurd or a waste of time – employers pay a lot of

money for the opportunity to use these types of activities and they take them seriously.

- Do suggest that the group nominates a time keeper and chairperson (if you are allowed) and keep an eye on the time yourself.
- Ask the people who have not spoken for a contribution.

The plot

. . . a series of challenges and situations from which you learn things about yourself and demonstrate your ability to achieve . . .

Another way in which your competencies will be tested is through the recruiters asking about them in the interview. Here your ability to demonstrate competencies takes the form of being able to tell a series of mini-anecdotes designed to reveal a moment when, for example, your capacity for initiative came to the fore in a real situation or when some character-building event led you to learn a valuable lesson about yourself (but from which you bounced back).

If they are talking about a holiday as an undergraduate and if you ask someone 'what kind of problems were there with that?', if someone actually says that it was all like clockwork, you know that they have either missed something or someone else has organized it for them, or they are trying to pretend that they are someone that they are not because we know that these things all have their glitches. What we are interested in is what the glitches were and how they identified and solved them. *(Consultancy)*

You will already have provided an example or two of this sort of thing on your application form and, as you can expect to be questioned on this example in your interview, you must re-read your application before the AC. However, you might also be asked to provide another example and you will certainly be asked to provide examples of key competencies. It is always better that these examples should come from a responsible work situation. However, if you cannot find anything truly responsible, then some sort of voluntary work, hobby or sports activity is nearly as good, while academic situations (teamwork in a research project, for example) come third. As with the application form, it is also important to use a range of examples.

In a commercial organization, the make-or-break competency can often be business awareness. All organizations differ slightly in how they interpret this, but it basically comes down to understanding that companies are there to turn a profit and that there is such a thing as internal politics.

We are looking for some kind of business commitment, so if you said you were applying to HR I want you to do more than just sit there and say that HR is about being with people . . . the interviewers are from the business area, they are very good at digging behind that. *(High street bank)*

Still one of the greatest reasons for lack of success at the selection process is a lack of commercial awareness. But that has got nothing to do with overall brightness, academic ability and the sorts of other selection criteria that are typically used. *(Consultancy)*

Tactics for interviews

The biggest danger for Players at the interview is the temptation to stretch the truth of your experience so far that it becomes a direct lie. At interview, direct lies are easy to spot because of the pressure of observation and the fact that the assessors have got so much experience examining graduates. And when they are spotted they are disastrous for your prospects. If you are a Player, you are much safer if you simply amplify or diminish aspects of your character and your experience according to the situation. 'Obviously I don't lie,' said one Player, 'but I think, to some extent, with interviews you have to play the game, so perhaps you might emphasize a part of your nature that isn't . . . make it more of a part of your nature, if you see what I mean.'

For another Player, who was present at a chemical manufacturer AC, it is a matter of how far she was prepared to go:

If I have a really strong thought on a certain answer then yes I'm me, if it is a really strong point about whether we should do animal tests or what have you, and I have a really strong view on that, and so the answer will be like, that's my answer. Whereas I think that with some answers you can be quite broad, so that you are not a definite no. Because I think that if you have a too strong, sensitive mind then, especially for the management schemes, I don't think they like you. I think for the first few [ACs] I didn't quite know what to be, so I was me, and now I tailor myself down slightly . . . For the management schemes, you have to be that sheep that they can, you know, they want to cut the wool off you to make you into whatever sort of shape they want.

Again, the biggest danger if you are a Purist is that in your attempt to come across as your natural self you will under-prepare your answers to those key competency questions. Without some sort of preparation, it is almost impossible to remember all of the situations you could use to demonstrate the required competencies and without this information at the forefront of your mind you are likely to walk away from the interview feeling that you have under-performed. As we have said before, as a Purist you must give just as polished a performance of your own (authentic) narrative of employ-ability as the Players do with their fake ones. One candidate put it like this: 'When they ask a question,' she said, 'I try and think straight away what competency they are looking for and then I give them an example to illustrate it.' All candidates, Players and Purists alike, should therefore do the following.

ESSENTIAL THINGS TO DO IN PREPARATION FOR INTERVIEW

- Re-read your application form or CV.
- Re-read the company literature where it explains which competencies they require.
- Prepare an example of each competency (and a back-up if you can).
- Make sure these examples come from a range of activities (employment, volunteering, travel, internships, hobbies, sports).
- Remember that employers are particularly looking for candidates who understand how the competencies relate to what the organization does – in a commercial organization business awareness is about understanding how the money is made.
- Do not tell a direct or verifiable lie.

The happy ending

. . . and a strong narrative drive towards a happy and satisfying ending

This completes the circle. The hero looks the part because he or she is the part. And his or her destiny is to end up as someone who works as a Y in organization X.

The final thing they will look for at an interview is the genuineness of your ambition. As we said in Part 1, part of the narrative of modern business, and an axiom of modern recruitment advice, is that it is not a job you are looking for but a way of life, even a vocation. You are, it is claimed, looking for the one unique economic role in which the potential of your unique combination of attributes can be fully realized. Whether you believe this or not, it is essential that you are seen to believe it. This is partly because of the strong cultural pressure that sees fulfilment as something that comes not from economic reward but from the delights of self-actualization, and partly it comes from the fact that your wanting to work for organization X flatters your interviewers as it means that you want to be like them.

More interview tactics

In order to convey the genuineness of your ambition, it is essential that you know a lot about organization X and are able to produce that information on demand. This sort of preparation will set you apart. Employers expect you to know it but, incredibly, many candidates fail to do this basic homework.

They know nothing about the company, nothing about the industry. 'What are the issues created in the industry?' 'Well customer service. Customer service because you have to be nice to your customers. Competition, because you get competition from other countries.' You don't even get the basics like the environment, and if fuel is going to run out. There is nothing even like that, never mind the more complicated things, which is they just look on the Net and see what they can find out and they are just horrendous when they come in . . . it's very easy to get information.

We do a few of the building relationships questions and part way down, what we call achievement orientation and I actually preface the question with 'You are not expected to get this one first but it is a very obvious question really, but why do you want to work for us?' 'I like cars!' You are just staggered by it. 'I have always liked cars, my dad drives [one of yours].' If you are lucky, you'll get 'You've got a really good training programme'. 'What makes you think that?' 'Umhh.'

And if you get a good one, the first answer 'I was really taken with the training programme, I'll take the personnel route. You do two six-month placements in two completely different areas within personnel. One is a line personnel role and the other is a central function so I would either be working in training or in the compensation area.' And it's brilliant . . . they just talk. They've thought about it. But so many of them haven't got a clue. We expect them to know a bit about the company and certainly to know why they want to work for us, and to know a bit about the issues that are facing us. If they don't, they've lost it at that point. They could have done really well in everything else, but it is based on that. *(Car manufacturer)*

ESSENTIAL THINGS YOU NEED TO KNOW FOR INTERVIEW

- The details of the graduate programme you have applied to.
- How it fits in with the other graduate programmes within the company.
- Why you applied for it (over its competitors).
- What the organization does.
- The names of its key products.
- Who its Chief Executive is.
- Who its stakeholders are.
- Its corporate strategy.
- Its marketing strategy.
- How it is financed.
- How many employees it has.
- Where it is based (nationally and internationally).
- Who its main competitors are.
- What its strengths and weaknesses are.
- The main issues facing the industry at the moment.

Tactics for the context in which you find yourself

However hard you prepare, the one thing you cannot plan for is the context you will find yourself in. You might not know how many jobs there are available, you certainly will not know the strengths and weaknesses of the other candidates, and you won't know the personalities of the assessors. This is important because so much of the result of an AC does turn on context.

If you look again at the candidate categories at the end of the facts section (see page 86), you will see that the difference between being a winner or a loser, a star or a razor for instance, is about perception (ignore the freezer/non-starter categories as neither of these get offered jobs). Remember that no one is a star in every context and no one is a razor in every context. Exactly the same behaviour can look good or bad depending on how many jobs there are, who the other candidates are, and what the attitudes of the individual assessors are on that day.

You can't control these things, but you can be aware of how your behaviour might be perceived in the context in which you find yourself. In the following example, the candidate seems to have misread, or perhaps not even thought about, mirroring the graduate brand through her clothing. She then did not have the presence of mind to adjust the way she presented herself to the context.

Some people wear the most inappropriate things to an assessment centre. We had an HR girl who had a gorgeous suit which was clearly very expensive, but it was cropped trousers, cropped top and she wore a really tiny vest top with no bra, so all the blokes couldn't wait to employ her. But then she was known as the shiny suit girl which isn't something you want to be known as. [This wasn't why she didn't get the job.] She terrified us. Her assertiveness skills were way over and she scared the group exercise people to death so she clearly wasn't appropriate. I did feed it back to her about her dress though because it was commented upon, never again, she bit my head off. She went wild. *(Telecoms company)*

Then again, when you have a lot of female assessors and a lot of female candidates, a male candidate who might look like something of a star in another context could, if he is too confident, start to come across as arrogant and so tip himself into the razor category.

How to be seen as a star and not a razor

While all employers are looking for confidence, the most important thing to avoid is any suggestion of arrogance towards the other candidates or the assessors. It is vital, therefore, that if you find yourself in a context in which you think yourself the best candidate you do not show this, and you must certainly never give the impression you have anything but respect for the assessors.

Will this person work well in a team? If he or she and you can have personalities which are very learned, have very strong opinions and the right opinions but they can be the brightest person in the world but if they are going to piss somebody off on the team then you don't want them on it, because it just won't work. *(IT consultancy)*

How to be a geek and not a nerd

Where there is a technical requirement for a job, it is possible that once you have seen the performance of other candidates you might start to worry that your technical or analytical skills will not be up to the mark. You might then start to try to compensate for this by pushing your technical experience at interview. Alternatively, you might find yourself the most technically qualified person there and so might emphasize your expertise in an attempt to mark yourself out from the other candidates. Both of these tactics may be mistakes. Your technical skills will almost certainly have been measured by one of the other more objective assessments. The difference between employable geeks and unemployable nerds doesn't come down to technical skills, it comes down to the ability to work with other people in teams. Emphasizing your team-working skills will probably be your best tactic in these circumstances.

How to be a safe bet and not an iffy

This is the most arbitrary distinction of them all. Whether to fit you into the first or the second of these categories is something that can take the assessors hours to decide so it is not something you are really going to be able to influence. Tactically, however, if you find yourself at an AC where there appear to be a lot of stars, you can assume that some of them are going to push the wrong buttons and come across as razors. Trying to keep up with this group might not therefore be your best option. Remember that all employers need safe, dependable people who can be relied on to do a decent job but who are never going to amaze. If you play up how steadily dependable you are, you might just take one of the job offers from one of the stars/razors.

Part

5

11

Strategies for the aftermath

This chapter is for the people who so far have not managed to live the dream and secure for themselves an aspirational graduate job. If you have been to a number of ACs but have yet to receive an offer, there are three things you can do. You can choose to stay in the game and keep on applying. You can take a break with the intention of returning in a year or so. Or you can choose to start focusing your ambitions elsewhere.

Strategies for staying in the game

If your intention is to keep going after rejection, the first thing you will need to do is to define your attitude to the feedback you will be offered. You need to ask yourself whether the feedback is merely providing an acceptable explanation for your rejection or whether it explicitly encourages you to reapply next year.

As we have suggested previously, some of the assessments, particularly the psychometric tests, are often used to provide a way of legitimizing decisions that have been made in other more instinctive and subjective ways. This is particularly true of feedback where the apparently objective measurements are used to provide an acceptable reason for rejecting you. This is what one employer had to say about it:

> ... the candidates want to know [why], and when you give them feedback it's about what they said and what they did. 'You didn't get through because the evidence around X wasn't so good, because you did Y, and you said Z.' You've got to be factual with them, you can't say, 'well actually when you came in the room we really didn't like the look of you.' *(High street bank)*

The truth is that the feedback, because it has to leave out these subjective human evaluations that are at the heart of graduate recruitment, is going to be less and less useful the closer you come to getting the job. Feedback that merely masks these subjective decisions and that does not suggest you should reapply should not be given much credence. However, if there is an explicit invitation to reapply, or if the feedback draws your attention to an objective weakness in your suitability, it does start to become useful. If you failed one of the objective aptitude tests, it might prompt you to prepare harder next time. If your attention is drawn to your performance in the group exercises, you could reconsider your strategies for these. The only real value to feedback is to use it as a way to sharpen your performance for the next AC, either for the same organization or for another one.

This is Gail, who, as a Player, uses the feedback strategically.

> I would be shocked if I didn't get through the next one now ... I asked them to ring me and tell me [why I didn't get in] and so I now know their scoring criteria. If they change it – and I don't think that will happen, I think they'll change the scenario but I can't really see them changing the scoring criteria, it's too expensive – I reckon I'll walk it. *(Gail)*

The idea of using feedback to improve your chances on reapplication is obvious Player behaviour, but it does not come easily to the Purists whose belief in the objectivity of the process tends to make them more accepting of the result. This is Douglas, contemplating whether or not he should reapply:

> I'll consider applying again once I get the feedback information to find out what they say. I'm not sure if I would, being honest, apply again, because I think if it's been . . . if I've not got in once the chances of me getting in a second time are very limited. Well, I think once you've applied once, if you don't meet the criteria once then unless you've done anything exceptionally different the second time I don't see how that could get you the place. I don't know, unless they drastically changed what they're looking for or the criteria that they're interested in, or things like that, I wouldn't see how it could. The way I look at it is if you don't fulfil the criteria once, are you likely to fulfil them a second time? *(Douglas)*

A Purist therefore, unless he or she failed because his or her mind went blank at a crucial point or for some other more or less accidental reason, is less likely to reapply than a Player. Once again, this is because the Purist views the result as objective while the Player sees a negative result simply as a learning experience from which to gain invaluable practice for the next audition.

Feedback aside, after a series of rejections, it may be necessary to reconsider your broader strategy. You should always remember that getting to an AC is in itself a considerable achievement. What it means is that you are very good at portraying the right narrative of employability on paper. However, if you have been rejected many times, it may be that you are less good at presenting the same narrative in person. If you have tried to be a Player and not succeeded, it may be that you should reconsider how convincing you really are and start to work more within the range of your real self. Yet Purists can fail because they have taken insufficient account of the fact that the narrative of employability has to be polished, however true to yourself it is. There are also likely to be some Purists who, after some bitter experience of the arbitrary nature of rejection, might shift to a Player approach.

After he had completed his AC, Terry received the following feedback: 'Terry gave a consistent performance over two days, which met our standard overall,' he was told. He then expected the next sentence to be the offer of a job, instead he heard this: 'But unfortunately we did see stronger candidates and are unable to offer Terry a position.'

As you may remember, Terry is a Purist and this made no sense:

You know, in my case, it has been four or five times now. It can be a bit demoralizing . . . I am not really happy with the kind of, you know the judgement that they have made and how they actually came to the decision. I just have a problem because what they say when you go into these assessment centres especially that you are working to a standard and that you are not competing against each other which, you know, brings about the atmosphere of people not really competing. So you are working to a standard, if you reach the standard you get a job. And so that is okay, that is a very clear-cut and defined thing.

Every assessment centre I have been to has said and this one was no different and so when you actually, when they say to you

'Oh you know you are up to the standard' and then you go 'okay fair enough'. And then when they say to you, you have reached the standard but you don't get the job because there were other stronger candidates there.

So in actual fact I am competing against other people, so once you get feedback like that, I think that is really subversive and ultimately you have actually got to think about how truthful they have been. That kind of just, you know, well they are basically not telling the truth. *(Terry)*

This is Terry, caught at the moment when he realizes he has been lied to about the AC. It *is* a competition. There is no objective pre-set standard. For all the camaraderie, for all the assessor and even senior management exhortations to be yourself and not think of it as a competition, this is exactly what it is. It is not an exam. It is not pass or fail depending on which standard you reach. It is a complex, positional game of winner-takes-all in which, if there are five places on the graduate training programme, five candidates will get them regardless of the fact that the sixth, seventh and eighth candidates would be, by any objective standard, equally good. However much potential you might have, if you are not in the first five, the gate will close in front of you.

We do not know whether Terry changed his strategy from Purist to Player as a result of his insight. However, there are always going to be ethical dimensions to the decision to change your strategy that cannot be ignored. Does success come naturally to those who deserve it as a result of their unique qualities? Or is it the prize in a Darwinian struggle for resources in which every advantage should be exploited to its maximum potential? This is a big question. There is no guide that can show you how to answer it for here is where you come up against your sense of self, your ambition, and your sense of right and wrong. There is only one thing to ask yourself, and it is an ethical question. How far are you prepared to go? Or to put it another way, how much of your sense of self and your integrity are you prepared to sacrifice to your ambition, and how much are you prepared to retain to remain true to who you really are?

Strategies for taking a break

A second response to rejection is to pull back and to take a break from the recruitment round for a while. Putting together a narrative of employability and performing it is not an easy thing to do if most of your experience has been limited to undergraduate education. The very act of gaining some experience in another area might be enough to help your awareness of, and your ability to construct, a narrative. The window of opportunity for entry onto a graduate training programme is actually quite long, around three to five years, starting from the final year of higher education, and it is possible to take a break. However, the temptation might be to think about this time merely as an opportunity to find yourself and discover what you really want to do with your life. Although this might be one benefit of a break, it should never be forgotten that employers are going to expect to see some skills gained from the things you decide to do. Employers are quite used to seeing periods of temping, further study and an extended period of travel on CVs. What they do not like to see, however, is anything that can be seen as drifting. If you want to return to the graduate market, it is essential that you give your period away from the job market a clear focus. Employers want to be able to make sense of what you are doing. You should focus your activity in such a way that it can link to a future narrative of employability. What you want to be saying in a year or two at interview is this: 'When I left university I realized I didn't have the skills that employers needed and I set about creating opportunities for myself to learn them.' Employers will love this.

Strategies for focusing on something else

Once you have entered the graduate recruitment market it is very easy to see it as the be-all and end-all of success. However, this is partly because of the marketing environment in which you find yourself. Graduate recruiting companies sell themselves as being an employment nirvana. Only with us, they claim, can you truly self-actualize, endlessly growing in knowledge, skills, self-awareness, and responsibility. This is not necessarily true. There are still many different paths to employment success and, although an aspirational graduate job may indeed be one of the quickest routes available to get you to the top, it is not a choice that is without its own difficulties. The number of people who down-size from graduate employment testifies to the price it can extract. It may be that if you have found the elite recruitment world of the AC a dispiriting place you may also find the world of elite employment similarly unfulfilling. Deciding to withdraw from the game altogether is not an ignoble option.

The final thing to say is that it is important not to allow a rejection or a series of rejections to define your sense of who you are. This is very easy to say, we know, but what this book should have done is given you a complete insight into exactly how arbitrary some of the recruitment industry's decisions can be. There are simply more good people than there are good jobs. And the more this is the case, the more the recruitment industry has to set up subjective and positional barriers. This is, in many ways, obvious and the only thing that obscures what is really going on is the recruitment industry's insistence that its decisions have to be seen as objective and justifiable. They are not. When there are over 400,000 graduates and only 15,000 aspirational graduate jobs, tens of thousands of equally able people are going to be rejected. We hope that what this book has done is reveal how and why this happens, and we hope that you now have good reason for understanding why rejection should never be seen as a definition of who you are.

Good luck with whatever you decide.